Praise for *Love, Death*

'Our family has always loved Nova Weetman's books ... Her observational powers are profound. In this book she turns them on herself, in an account of what it is to be a grown-up and lose the person you've loved best. Weetman stares with composure, honesty and curiosity into the face of pain, despair and loneliness – and what she finds is rich and complex. It's a beautiful, generous book ... This book feels like a companion.'

Annabel Crabb

'As much a map of grief as it is a vast vessel of profound love. As much about the cruelty of lives cut unfairly short as it is about how those lives transform us. This is a moving, tender and loving book.'

Benjamin Law

'This is a devastatingly beautiful exploration of life, love and loss, from a brilliant writer who found the courage to share the most difficult parts of her life. An exceptional book.'

Myf Warhurst

'This book is so special. Nova Weetman writes like Helen Garner makes me feel. I was slowly but surely submerged into the world that she creates and, by the time I realised, it was too late and I was wholly inside. *Love, Death & Other Scenes* is a treasure.'

Jacinta Parsons

'Written with such beauty and honesty. I felt as if I knew these people to the core, and now profoundly miss them.'

Melina Marchetta

Nova Weetman is a widely published writer of fiction, nonfiction and screenplays. She has published eighteen novels for children about friendship, class, identity and belonging, and her books have been shortlisted for many awards and published internationally. Her recent essays on aspects of grief and loss have been published in *The Guardian*, *The Age* and *Island* literary magazine, leading to her appearing on Radio National's *Conversations*. Nova has also published short fiction in *Island*, *Mslexia*, *Kill Your Darlings* and *Overland*, and worked as a screenwriter for television and film.

Love, Death & Other Scenes

a memoir

Nova Weetman

UQP

First published 2024 by University of Queensland Press
PO Box 6042, St Lucia, Queensland 4067 Australia

The University of Queensland Press (UQP) acknowledges the Traditional Owners and their custodianship of the lands on which UQP operates. We pay our respects to their Ancestors and their descendants, who continue cultural and spiritual connections to Country. We recognise their valuable contributions to Australian and global society.

uqp.com.au
reception@uqp.com.au

Copyright © Nova Weetman 2024
The moral rights of the author have been asserted.

This book is copyright. Except for private study, research, criticism or reviews, as permitted under the Copyright Act, no part of this book may be reproduced, stored in a retrieval system, or transmitted in any form or by any means without prior written permission. Enquiries should be made to the publisher.

Cover design by Josh Durham, Design by Committee
Cover illustration by Bren Luke
Typeset in 12/17 pt Bembo Std by Post Pre-press Group, Brisbane
Printed in Australia by McPherson's Printing Group

University of Queensland Press is assisted by the Australian Government through Creative Australia, its principal arts investment and advisory body.

This project is supported by the Victorian Government through Creative Victoria.

A catalogue record for this book is available from the National Library of Australia

ISBN 978 0 7022 6843 4 (pbk)
ISBN 978 0 7022 6960 8 (epdf)
ISBN 978 0 7022 6961 5 (epub)

University of Queensland Press uses papers that are natural, renewable and recyclable products made from wood grown in well-managed forests and other controlled sources. The logging and manufacturing processes conform to the environmental regulations of the country of origin.

To A, E and A. Always.

Contents

Prologue: Farewell	1

Act One: Love

Scene One: The Heartbreak Choir	11
Scene Two: Writers	18
Scene Three: Ambition	30
Scene Four: Bowerbirds	42
Scene Five: Soundtrack	54
Scene Six: Family	61
Scene Seven: Memento Mori	68

Interval One: A Photograph in Time	83

Act Two: Death

Scene One: Diagnosis	87
Scene Two: Shame	95
Scene Three: A Tabby	106
Scene Four: Lasts	116
Scene Five: Kissing	123
Scene Six: Goodbyes	134
Scene Seven: And the Light Goes Out	142

Interval Two: Untitled   151

Act Three: Other Scenes
    Scene One: No Time for Rituals   155
    Scene Two: Grief   162
    Scene Three: Mourning   170
    Scene Four: Gone   177
    Scene Five: Homeowner   186
    Scene Six: Hypochondria   196
    Scene Seven: Stuff   202
    Scene Eight: Isolation   212
    Scene Nine: This or Death   223
    Scene Ten: Birthday   231
    Scene Eleven: Grass Widow   244
    Scene Twelve: Single   255
    Scene Thirteen: Company   265

Epilogue: In the Gaps   273

Author's Note   278

Prologue: Farewell

Organising a memorial for you is a little like organising the opening night of one of your plays. I must find a venue, cast the leads, arrange finger food, stump up cash for the bar, choose songs for after the formalities and write the program.

It takes fifteen months to organise because Covid lockdowns keep interrupting and I move the date many times. We never actually talked about what you wanted. All I know is that it will be far away from the nearest Catholic church. But I don't need you here for that decision.

I think you'd like something theatrical, so I book the ballroom down the road. You know the one – we went a couple of times, saw some bands. One of the kids had a school concert there and we sat together near the front, holding hands.

I realise as I make plans that our celebrations have always occurred in fragments. Opening nights with your theatre friends. Book launches with mine. Dinners with smaller groups. Birthdays with some but not all. This will be a coming together of everyone we know and love.

And the only person missing will be you.

I pick that photograph of you in your baby-blue glasses for the little service handbook. The one I took on the canal boat in Venice, years back now, when the kids were both in primary school. You treasure those glasses. I've kept them for you. One of your friends say they look like something his nanna would wear. You would laugh at that.

Organising a memorial is sort of like hosting a sad wedding. Contacting all those people. Working out who will speak, who will sing. Our friends all rally, divvying up jobs and helping without needing to be asked. They write tributes and songs, speeches and door lists. Others cook food to serve after the proceedings to save me money. It takes me back to those early years at Chameleon Theatre when you produced a play on a dime.

The song list is tackled by our eldest. She adds in all your favourites. Songs I can never remember the names of. They are all there: Willie Nelson, Jim Croce, Dinosaur Jr., Elliott Smith, a smattering of Morrissey, and some Nina Simone and Cat Power to break up all the men. She knows you so well. You would probably sing along or maybe dance later in the night when people loosen up after they've cried.

I have fifteen months to write your eulogy and yet I circle. I don't know how to sum up all those years with you. We were two weeks shy of twenty-five years together when you died. Not that we would have celebrated our anniversary. We weren't great at that, were we?

Prologue

Each time I sit down to write, I keep imagining you saying Ben Stiller's line from *Zoolander* about being a eugooglizer, one who speaks at funerals. I remember you watching that with the kids and giggling at every joke.

You store up your giggles for silly films. Like that night at the cinema when you laughed so loud, you shot popcorn out of your mouth into the hair of the person sitting in front. And we spent the next two hours trying to work out what to do about it.

I'm sorry, but I don't know how to say everything about you. I write about seeing you for the first time in the window of an op shop all those years ago. About your love of second-hand things and rescuing stuff from the side of the road. I weave in our kids, the ups, the downs, your love of lamps and your hat collection. And then, I find myself wondering what you'd say about me if I was gone.

How do you love me?

On the bus heading across town to see Dad, I read *Oh William!*, a book by Elizabeth Strout. Do you remember how I watched her speak online from the other side of the world for a writers' festival event when you were bedridden? You called out as she was mid-sentence and I came in to tell you that I thought she was very similar to you in the way you found story in people. You wanted to know more but we had to wait until the oxycodone kicked in and eased your pain, and then I explained how she'd talked about finding one of her characters as she unpacked the dishwasher.

You smiled. That was all. Just a smile. But I knew it meant you understood.

In the book I read on the bus, she reaches into me and finds my grief. I shudder, tears collect and I stare from the window to find something else to focus on. If you were with me, you would hand me one of your square blue cotton handkerchiefs.

The part that makes me cry is when the main character talks about why she fell in love with her ex-husband William. How when she first met him, it was his sense of authority that made her love him. The fact that she knew just by looking at him that he may do what was asked of him, but no-one would ever have his soul.

Reading these words on the Punt Road hill, I understand that was what I saw through the window that day I first saw you, when I watched you try on an overcoat. And that is one of the things I love most about you. The sense that you know yourself. That you will never compromise parts of yourself for anyone. Sometimes that leads to us arguing because I feel frustrated by your stubbornness. But I think it's as much your signature identity as your brown felted hat is.

I'm not sure I ever told you that, so I want you to know now.

The days leading up to the memorial are messy. You can imagine. I buy our son two second-hand suits to choose from. One quirky and odd – blue checks and too short, exposing his ankles. The other dark and adult. He chooses the blue checks and finds one of your black shirts that sits too large on his boy-sized body. I can't quite watch him dressing to farewell you. But he looks so sharp – like a mini-you.

Our daughter chooses a black fitted dress that I wore to the

Prologue

opening night of one of your plays. And I buy a delicate top – sheer and spotted. We each have our outfits. New skins in which to face the world.

When I arrive home from the sound check to collect our kids, our son is dressed and ready and wearing one of your hats. I am surprised that it fits him because I didn't know your heads were the same size. Yours always seems so … large.

As we rush around doing last-minute jobs, the three of us don't talk much. The weight of the day is heavy. We need you here, cracking jokes.

We buy up hundreds of mini-packets of chicken chips to scatter on the tables. I'm still strictly a cheese-and-onion girl myself, but you love chicken until the end.

I have my hair done for you. Styled in a salon. You would laugh and tell me to save the money, probably offer to straighten it for me. Like you always offer to build me a table out of used toilet rolls. You hate spending money on things you can do yourself.

I'm not sure why I have it styled. These days, my hair mostly sits wild and uncombed, a mass of dry and forgotten straw-like ends. But on this day, I keep touching it, surprised by how soft it feels.

On the street, walking to the ballroom, we run into some of your family on their way there. The sprawling, dark-haired collective that looks almost cult-like en masse. There are some hugs and some not because Covid still looms for us all.

The kids and I walk up the stairs to the venue in a line of follow the leader. We show our vaccination certificates on our phones. We stick on smiles and stand together at the top of the stairs greeting people as they arrive. The three of us, like we are okay.

You would comment on your lovely little family if you saw us. Say it in a voice that reveals how emotional you are at the thought that the two of us became a four. You never stop marvelling at that.

We hand out the flyers my brother has made about the order of service – your face wryly smiling on the cover, your words on the back from one of the scenes in your play *The Architect*.

More people hug us. It has been nearly two years without hugs and now people hug us. No masks. Just arms and words and smiles and the squeezing of shoulders. Our kids greet people like it is their duty. I tell them that it's not, that they can retreat. But they stay firmly by my side.

Nobody can see that we are drowning inside.

Someone hands our son a pint of lemonade. He drinks it too fast. Our daughter leaves to find her people. And then, in the heaving room, I lose them both. I haven't been in a crowd for so long. And there are hundreds here. You would be surprised by all the faces. People you haven't seen in years turn up to farewell you, their old friend.

It is like being at a party where the guest has forgotten to arrive. Everyone is waiting for you. And you are nowhere and everywhere. In all the conversations. In all the memories. But gone too.

When it is time for the ceremony part, I stand down the front at the side because I am speaking. And because I am trying to avoid the tears at the back of the room.

I search for our kids in the crowd. Our daughter sits halfway back with her friends, a table of teenage strength. Our son is down the front with your old friends and his too. Three boys in clean clothes, looking respectful and out of place.

Your middle brother takes to the stage first to tell the story

Prologue

of the child you once were. He is funny and real, like you. Your eldest sister offers him support and reads an Irish blessing. Then your writer friends speak about your work, your humour, your brain. They are erudite and impressive and make others in the room wish they had writer friends too, someone to eulogise them when they are gone.

Then the triple act of women who have been your besties for many years weave a speech together of anecdotes. You were once formidable as a four, they are now lessened as a three. It doesn't seem right you aren't up there with them, speaking too.

There are laughs and stories and songs from dear friends who love you. And I hear all and none. When it is my turn to speak, I read from the pages I've printed, hoping it explains what I feel about you. I am honest. About us. About you.

The choir you joined take us out. And your friend has cut together a montage of video clips from all the television shows you were in when you still acted – the purple-cloaked cult leader in *Neighbours*, the bogan barfly in *Blue Heelers*, the childlike fool in Russell Coight's *All Aussie Adventures*. There are more laughs.

People drink when it is over. They eat the food our friends have made. I sip at champagne and avoid conversation, offering up a quick word or two but not managing much else.

The faces of our past are present. I introduce our son to people he knows from the television and he giggles. A friend jokes that if the room explodes, there will be no more entertainment in Melbourne because everyone is here.

At some point our son starts vomiting on the balcony. Nerves and lemonade. A friend cleans it up and my brother takes him home.

Our daughter disappears with her friends and I can't find her. I wish I could leave too.

The perfect send-off, people say. And it is. It's like you're in the room. But you aren't.

I'm floating somewhere else and I can't imagine what it is like for our kids to hear all those things about you — their dad — the man they know best. To hear people claiming you and laying out stories of you whose life did not begin with theirs. So many stories of you they don't know.

I farewell others heading to the pub to continue reminiscing about you and walk home alone, avoiding the drunk man on the corner who calls out something.

I ring our daughter. She says she will be home soon. It is late. I tell her I'll come and collect her, but she doesn't want me to.

Our son has stopped vomiting when I arrive. In fact, he is hungry. I make him a Vegemite and butter sandwich, heavy on the butter.

I ring our daughter again. Tell her she needs to come home. I am starting to worry.

It is another hour before she appears. She shuts her bedroom door.

Our son does too.

And I go to bed, the cat taking up your side, stretching out and curling against me like she is mimicking you.

Act One:
Love

Scene One:
The Heartbreak Choir

When Aidan died, I inherited his tax bill and his estate. Now, I am the keeper of the keys. The holder of the copyright of his work. The person who must sign off on casting and script decisions. And yet I know nothing about theatre. It has never been my domain. I sit in the dark with the rest of the audience, transfixed by what unfolds before me, but I do not understand the backstage.

Aidan wrote many plays in his career. He also directed some and starred in the earlier ones when he ran a theatre company with two of his friends. As his career grew, his plays became more ambitious in scope and style, moving away from the one-act, hour-long pieces to large-scale, main-stage productions.

Following the success of his play *The Architect* in 2018, he wanted his next work to be a comedy. His intention was to write a trilogy – *The Architect* was the tragedy, the second was the comedy and the third, which would never eventuate, would be satire.

Around this time, we went to see our daughter's music concert at her high school. She was in one of the choirs and they were performing an arrangement of a song by legendary Melbourne composer and choir director Sue Johnson. As we worked our way through a bag of chips that we'd brought along in lieu of dinner, the choir sang – a wash of forty young voices, woven together.

That was the moment Aidan decided singing was what he'd been missing.

The next week, he went with a friend to a rehearsal of the Pagan Angels, one of the many choirs Sue Johnson leads in Melbourne. He came home calm and smiling and a little smug. Apparently, he had a lovely tenor voice and, besides, they needed men.

Aidan had never been a joiner. He avoided groups of people with names he knew he'd likely forget as soon as they parted. He left the school council meetings and the netball coaching to me. But the choir was different. He felt restored.

Each Thursday night he headed off to the Abbotsford Convent to sing in tune. He became one of those born-again choir members, telling everyone they needed to sing. Initially he even tried with me, but no amount of his private coaching could help my voice over the line. In our house, I've always been the family joke when it comes to music – the only person not a member of a choir, the only person who can't hold a note, the only person without any musical talent at all except for a little year-eight flute. Our children have been blessed with Aidan's musical genes. They both play multiple instruments and can recognise a song in seconds.

Pagan Angels wasn't just about the singing for Aidan. It was about being vulnerable, being honest with the people he met. Through the act of trusting each other with song, they spoke of their lives. And he felt safe, changed by the communal act of sharing his voice.

And then he was diagnosed.

When he came to write his new play, the comedy in his trilogy, he turned to his Thursday night choir and found his story. One of hope and humour in a small town. A play about the past and the damage of the church, and ultimately about the power of singing. He recognised that his own need to come together and sing with people, who started as strangers and slowly became friends, would be the heart of it.

And then he started missing choir because he was in pain or having treatment. I urged him to keep going, knowing how it made him feel. But he was torn. Aidan always processed things alone. He wasn't like me. He didn't just spew his feelings out to the person standing closest. He kept them tight, making sense of them first before returning to the world. And choir was somewhere he couldn't hide. In many ways it was one of the most regular outings of his week, aside from chemo or visiting the oncologist. So the choir members saw him struggle, even if they didn't know the details.

In November 2019, Aidan was due to sing the lead of the Nick Cave & The Bad Seeds song 'Into My Arms' for a Pagan Angels performance at the Abbotsford Convent. Finally, the kids and I would see him sing. That Saturday morning, I was setting up a toy stall in the school gym for our son's primary school fete. The plan was the kids and I would go to the convent that afternoon and watch the performance and then all go out for dinner.

I was knee-deep in bright-coloured plastic when Aidan found me in the school gym. He was pale. Two rounds into chemotherapy and it was knocking him. He was wearing my mum's old green raincoat that always looked so out of place on him with its cheery colour and its oversized shape.

I stopped sorting jigsaw puzzles to make plans about where to meet at the convent. He started crying in the gym and told me not to come. He didn't want us there. He wouldn't be able to sing if we watched him. I didn't understand. I thought we helped when he felt vulnerable and shaky, but he said it was too much.

He left and I went back to pricing Barbies.

That was the only public performance Aidan did with the Pagan Angels. I have a recording of it. His voice is strong. Sometimes when I'm trying to find him now in the house, I play it and the layer of thirty voices harmonising helps. He is singing the solo and, each time I hear it, I can imagine him that day without us, trying to make it to the end of the song without breaking down.

I don't have text messages or voicemail messages from him where he says my name because my phone died not long after he did and took them all with it.

But I have him singing.

He spent hours talking with Sue at the Pagan Angels about his play. She helped him understand choirs and how they work. Writing kept him focused on something other than medicine and hospital appointments. It gave us an engine to our family that wasn't just about him being sick.

In the foreword to the play, he writes: *The reason for the choir to exist was about wanting culture and beauty. It was about finding joy. But it was mostly about finding a connection that wasn't transactional and wasn't sport.*

Act One: Love

He finished writing that play, *The Heartbreak Choir*, in late 2019 and it was programmed for the following year, April 2020. Aidan went to a reading with the cast and came home exhausted. Sitting in a chair for hours with cancer in his spine was painful and hard. We weren't talking about the play as if it would be his last, even though we both knew.

Then Covid hit and theatres in Melbourne went dark. The play, like so many others, had to be cancelled. We were devastated but hopeful that if it was programmed in 2021, he'd be alive to see it.

But he wasn't.

Then the play was rescheduled for April 2022. Given that Covid battered the things we looked forward to for years, I was determined not to think about it. I chose to treat it like an unreliable friend who might or might not turn up for dinner.

When rehearsals started, the director, one of Aidan's closest friends and someone who knows Aidan's work better than I do, called to ask me about changes to the script. I told him I trusted him. Part of me wanted to step away from the work, fearful of how it would feel to be close to it without Aidan.

The first season of a new play is an important one. The play will change and fatten over the rehearsal process as the writer sits in, observing what works and what doesn't.

It is a living thing. Perhaps like the editing process for a book.

But this play had no author. He was gone. It was a first season of a new work and the writer was an empty chair.

Before he died, Aidan talked about his legacy or, more specifically, about not leaving one. I tried to comfort him, reassure him that in fact his work was his legacy, and his children. He was on increasing doses of oxycodone and steroids, and confused at times about things, but the thought that he was leaving us with nothing was a repeating fear.

The Heartbreak Choir did premiere in April 2022. On the opening night at the Melbourne Theatre Company, it stormed. Terrified we'd arrive late, I did an illegal U-turn in the city, much to the kids' horror, and clipped the bottom of the car on a concrete bollard, dinting a panel. One friend was caught in the storm and turned up drenched, while I had to dry my hair under the hand-dryer in the theatre bathroom.

The company had kept a chair empty towards the front of the theatre, signalling the concept of Aidan. Until the lights went down, I kept sneaking glances at that chair, like the ghost of him could sense we were nearby.

Sitting surrounded by friends in a theatre full of people who understood that Aidan was gone, I reached for the hands of our children. As the lights went down, I realised I was holding my breath. My shoulders were tense and high. I couldn't settle.

What would this audience make of Aidan's work?

Within five minutes of the actors taking the stage, people started to laugh. I tried to laugh too, but I kept hearing his voice. Like a painter's brushstrokes, writers have idiosyncratic ways of using language. Aidan's is comedic and sharp and I could hear him cracking jokes with the kids, laughing with his siblings, his friends. The dialogue was like a patchwork of our lives.

By interval, I was almost breathing steadily. As we filed out of the theatre, a song came on and I realised it was one my daughter had picked for the playlist she'd devised of Aidan's favourites:

Act One: Love

The Smiths, Wings, Jim Croce and Willie Nelson. His regular soundtrack.

I smiled, wondering how often Melbourne Theatre Company audiences heard Morrissey singing as they left the theatre. Weaving through the crowd, I made it to the bar for a double Scotch on the rocks, which I drank too fast. I was like a floating narrator, overseeing everything, eavesdropping on conversations, checking to see if people liked it, so I could go back home and report to him.

I saw the play seventeen times over the next four weeks. Whenever I was missing him, I'd duck in and watch a performance. I sat in different spots in the theatre, with different eyelines and different views. The cast changed as Covid hit and took actors out for a week at a time. The season even closed for a few nights because of it. I'd never watched a play so many times before. I'd never needed to.

But for the six weeks that the season ran, it was like he was there. His fingers gripping my knee as I listened to the actors say his words, him whispering in the dark to check that I liked it. If he'd been alive, it would have been him watching the play over and over and over to see what he could cut, what line wasn't working, how the play might evolve. But that was my job now. To watch over it, to be its parent, its advocate.

As the play now slowly settles into productions in other cities – Auckland and Sydney to come – I will see it again and again, remembering lines and loving characters, and all the while wishing I could whisper back in the dark, that *yes, yes, yes, I love it.*

Scene Two:
Writers

It was no accident that I fell in love with a writer. At eighteen, I moved from the outer-eastern suburbs of Melbourne into the inner city, trying on a new version of myself. Wearing tartan skirts and op-shopped cardigans, I began reading Sylvia Plath poetry on the weekends, daring to believe I was the first to discover her.

From the age of seven, writing was all I ever really wanted to do. Throughout my childhood, I wrote to my dad's friend. We had adopted character roles for our letters – she was Ms Gumble and I was Ms Bottersnike – our names taken from my favourite book *Bottersnikes and Gumbles* by SA Wakefield. The Bottersnikes were lazy, ugly creatures who never appreciated the Australian bush. But the Gumbles tried to clean up, removing rubbish and caring for the land. The conservation message washed over me as a child. Rather, I just liked that the Gumbles outwitted, outplayed and outlasted those Bottersnikes every single time.

Act One: Love

I still have Ms Gumble's letters, some typed and some handwritten. I marvel now at her patience as she wrote many times to a child she wasn't even related to.

Throughout school, I was always being told that I could write. Talented at English, I could whip out something half decent in a matter of hours. But I was lazy, preferring to try on the identity of a writer without ever writing very much at all. I thought that writing was something that happened to you. Like a Christmas miracle. You woke up one day and you were an author. No effort required.

After I moved out of home, there were many rituals required before I could sit down to write. The stovetop pot of coffee stolen from my parents' house would need to percolate. I would need to drink one or maybe two cups. Talk to my housemates about the dreams we'd had and analyse all of them. In detail. Talk about my novel that I hadn't started. And make plans for the evening.

By lunchtime, I might have written a line or maybe a page and then I'd start most of those rituals again. But I couldn't make it past page fifty-five.

When I met Aidan, he was already a real artist – writing, directing, performing, producing. He had his own theatre company and reviews in the paper. Four years older and more successful than me, I trailed behind him, struggling to keep up. I tried writing plays but could never work out how to get actors on and off the stage.

Around this time, I wrote a short story about a Polish man who'd lost his hearing during the war and avoided the trauma that sound caused by leaving wads of gauze buried in his ear canals.

It was accepted for publication in an anthology and I then adapted it as a short film that Aidan later directed.

It was the only time our collaboration led to a finished piece of work and it was a success. *Mr Wasinski's Song* was haunting. Sixteen minutes long with almost no dialogue, it won awards and took us overseas to festivals. We had ambitious plans to make more and started working on similarly sad stories of loss, but we kept missing out on much-needed funding rounds.

Eventually, Aidan drifted back to theatre and I started working in television to pay the rent. Working in different mediums, we were out of sync with each other. One on the up, one on the down. Never flying at the same time.

When I moved in with him in 1997, we converted the second bedroom into an office where we could both write. His play *Chilling and Killing My Annabel Lee* was being performed across the country. It was inspired by Edgar Allan Poe and it was a complex literary whodunnit, with a miserable policeman at its core. He dedicated it to his parents in that way that young artists do.

The day he received his first big royalty cheque, he rang to tell me he'd banked twenty-five thousand dollars, which to us seemed like lottery money. Until then we'd lived on snatches of work, tiny payments that we would stretch out for weeks, until we ran out of food and he would start eating dinner at the bar where he worked and I would return to visiting my parents for a proper meal.

When the cheque cleared, I was in Sydney visiting an old friend and doing work experience on a television show. I went shopping with my friend in Bondi and bought a pair of black-and-white pinstriped pants that I'd tried on about fifteen times before and had resisted buying because they were so expensive. Aidan and I had agreed that whenever we were properly paid for our work, we would each buy something that we loved.

I still have these pants. Pure wool, they give a little, so I can squeeze into them at a pinch, worrying they may split a seam if I bend over too fast. My daughter has borrowed them a couple of times and begs me to let her wear them more often, but they represent so much of those days that I can't quite let them go. Our hopes for success. My first grown-up purchase. An endless sense of longing. They are the pants of a playwright's girlfriend. Tailored and sharp, they attended many an opening night. Now, they hang in my wardrobe, waiting and remembering.

Around that time, I started sending letters overseas to film directors I admired, asking for work experience. Hal Hartley's 'no' came with three typed lines and two frames of film from his masterpiece *Trust*. Francis Ford Coppola's arrived with a monogrammed baseball cap. Spielberg's company sent a letter explaining that if his film coincidentally used the same story as the one that I'd sent, then he couldn't be sued. That confused me because I hadn't sent him a story. Just a short letter explaining who I was and a CV with almost nothing on it.

It's nearly impossible in this country to live as an artist, to make your income from the skill you have perfected over many years. Most of us work multiple jobs, masquerading as bartenders, waiters, teachers, shitkickers. Our egos are so broken by the need to do anything to pay the rent that it takes a lot to then put your art on the line for more rejection.

And there was a lot of rejection in those years. I used to joke about having an exhibition called *NO* featuring all the letters I'd received. To keep on believing in your work when there are daily reminders that you aren't good enough, aren't what they want, aren't young enough, aren't old enough, aren't something enough, is very tiring.

I'm now more robust about rejection, but back then, when I was surrounded by jobbing artists who were quick-witted and funny, I felt panicked at my lack of ideas. And instead of writing, I worried.

It was years later that I started the slog. The words on the page each day. The acceptance that it might not be the first book, the second book or even the third that would be published. And that was when I began to realise how hard writing was. How desperate it made you at times, and how miserable.

And yet we couldn't walk away. Aidan spent months railing about theatre every year. It was like the lover who broke his heart almost weekly, but he couldn't leave. It was up to me to bolster him. It was up to him to do the same for me.

Then, after my first agent failed to sell my adult literary novel and my second languished in the top drawer, even Mum started to develop doubts, politely suggesting I retrain. The house we were renting wasn't that far from the public housing she had grown up in. We had a resident rat in the pantry, an outdoor shower and gaps under the doors that had to be filled with blankets in winter because of the endless draught.

But we were in our late twenties and we were artists. We filled that house with hard rubbish, found furniture and hand-me-downs from friends with real jobs. I started working as a publicist

Act One: Love

three days a week at a cinema, trying to write in my spare time. Aidan was travelling the country, directing and writing plays for any theatre company that would have him. We were busy and relatively happy. The fact that we could live in a suburb that didn't judge our second-hand ways was a win.

I know that Mum had hoped for a different life for her daughter who'd gone to university. That she had believed I would live up to more than she feared she had. She'd climbed so hard from the poverty she was born into and she couldn't settle the thought that I'd willingly gone back.

Two writers in a house without income and security should have meant tension. But it didn't. After we had children, we would battle over time to write and who deserved more of it, but back then, in that early stage of love and nesting, we just hoped.

The year Mum died from cancer, I signed with a new agent who negotiated a two-book deal for me with a publisher. Mum never knew. She wasn't there at my book launch in 2014, proudly listening as my debut young adult novel, *The Haunting of Lily Frost*, was released into the world.

Aidan wasn't there either. He was directing a play in Tasmania and we couldn't afford the airfare for him to fly home. But friends and family came. Mum's besties, who'd known me since I was a baby, and all the people who'd listened patiently to my writing dreams crowded into the bookshop to hear my nervous first public reading. The signing queue snaked around in a looping circle and I grinned for nearly an hour as I scrawled out a message on each book.

I don't know why things worked out like that. At the time I wondered if Mum dying gave me the push to write without her support. If it made me chase a real audience. One that would pay. Or if it was just bad luck.

Aidan was my fixer of stories. Always. We would sit down over many coffees and I'd talk, telling him the problems. He would help me find where it had gone wrong. It was usually structure, something I don't care for, even now. It's big-picture writing and I struggle to grasp all the thoughts in my head. Instead, I chase the small – the characters, their worlds and why they do what they do. But he could tell, just by listening to me, where the story sagged or needed more.

He didn't read much of my work, not the books anyway. He said it was because he was an undiagnosed dyslexic. He took months to read a novel, where I would skip through a pile of books in the same time. The books he did read, he committed almost to memory. Vladimir Nabokov's *Lolita*, Thornton Wilder's *The Bridge of San Luis Rey*. I wanted him to be a reader, to share in the worlds that writers create, but he just wasn't.

I read his drafts though, listened as he fleshed out characters and themes. But he didn't need me like I needed him. I was a sounding board, a voice of encouragement, a trainer mopping his head when he was on the ropes. But I never gave him the formula to a knockout punch. He did that work himself.

Aidan had an ear for dialogue but was dreadful at spelling. When our daughter quizzed him once on how to spell 'pigeon', he sang out the letters adding a 'd' in the middle, and she laughed, thinking he was being funny.

I was his first reader, but not for story. Just for spelling, grammar

Act One: Love

and layout. And sometimes for reassurance. Each time he wrote a play, I would have to fix all the mentions of 'won't', because he jammed the apostrophe between the 'o' and the 'n'. I still remember explaining that the apostrophe was for the missing letter and he was amazed that he'd never been taught that.

I'd grown up my father's child, coming from generations of grammar pedants. At a recent Christmas gathering, my cousin announced that this year there would be no spelling bee. This year it would be a quiz instead. He then went on to explain that the gathered family members were all grammar pedants and spelling bees became too competitive and my son rejoiced. He is like his dad.

My grandfather used to read the *Macquarie Dictionary* cover to cover and write to them with suggested corrections. My dad has been known to avoid a particular café because of the spelling of 'cuppoccino' on the board out the front.

And here I was loving a man who cared little for being grammatically correct. It was always about story.

Aidan wrote slowly and usually only wrote one or two drafts, sitting down at the computer after months of imagining in his head. The play he sent off to the theatre company would change very little between him writing it and what was performed on opening night. He was confident about his work, ready to fight for it if he had to.

Here he is being interviewed about his process for the Melbourne Theatre Company:

> I will clean the entire house before sitting down to write a single line. I used to berate myself for that. Now I just tell

myself I'm not ready yet and that things are still cogitating. This means that when I do sit down to write I write fast, often getting out a first draft in a week. This means I'm totally immersed and not hopping in and out of the 'world'. I also try not to revise during this stage. I rarely cut. I never cut and paste. I just want to get the thing down organically and then see what I've got. There's a great joy to be had doing it this way. Analysis can come later.

I write fast and messy and without direction, needing to redraft and redraft and redraft before I find the kernel. And even then, I listen eagerly when my editor tells me what isn't working and what needs to go.

He loved language and the beats of dialogue. I love emotion and how a character feels.

When I talk to a friend about how Aidan processed his life, I realise he approached writing in the same way. He never fleshed out his feelings over months of conversations. He went inward until he'd found his resolution and he only talked about it once it had shape. Perhaps that explains why I write the way I do, given that I use my friends, and once used Aidan, to thrash out ideas and meaning before I can understand.

We were never in competition with each other, but I'm not sure I always felt his literary equal. It wasn't his doing; he had my back. It was this nagging feeling that as an author of children's and young adult books, I wasn't as real as him. His work was performed overseas, won awards and earned him a reputation.

Act One: Love

He was a successful writer of plays for the Australian mainstage. He wrote for adults.

I did not.

Even after publishing many books, securing an audience and being deeply proud of my work, I don't always feel legitimate among authors of adult books. Perhaps because, to them, I am an unknown quantity, possibly recognised if they have a child of a certain age who likes reading contemporary drama, but more likely an author of work they have never heard of.

We talk about this a lot in the kid-lit world, this feeling that we are somehow visitors to a writing community that doesn't always take us seriously. It may explain why we are supportive of each other. That's not to say we aren't envious sometimes. That all comes with the territory of being an artist in a country too small to support all of us. But mostly we are happy if somebody breaks through or, in the words of my writer friends, 'if someone has their Graeme Base *Animalia* moment' – a book that has sold more copies than any of us can dream of.

I'd failed to publish two adult novels when I started writing a teenage friendship story called *Frankie and Joely*. I thought I was still writing for grown-ups, but my agent disagreed – *Frankie and Joely* would go on to be published as my second young adult novel in 2015. It is not a book that sold particularly well, but it is a book that I love. The only third-person novel I have published, it is a coming-of-age story that switches perspective between five characters constantly so the reader knows exactly what this group of young people think of each other.

I'd always thought that being published would instantly change my life. It didn't. My first book came out. It sold a few thousand copies and had some okay reviews but once the excitement had settled down, I realised I had to go and do it all over again. And again. And again.

And for the chance to be published again and again, I'm very grateful. I love writing for young people and believe in the power of getting the right book into the hands of a child at the right time. I love the immediate response you get from children and young adults. The declarations of 'You're my favourite author' and the equal number of kids telling you why they don't like your work at all. I love the friends I've made, the publishers and editors I've worked with, the characters I've created in big groups of rowdy year sixes. I love the storytelling and the remembering back to who I was when I was thirteen. And I love the books that I have written.

But if I'm honest, sometimes I also wanted a bit of what Aidan had. I wanted to grapple with the big questions. I wanted to swear on the page and not take it out for fear of losing sales in schools. I wanted to write about sex and religion and class and fury and all the things that don't belong in a book for readers aged between ten and fourteen.

I was a little in awe of what Aidan could do and sometimes hoped his talent would rub off on me.

In 2018 when he was already diagnosed and had started chemotherapy and his skin was yellowing and puffy, we went to the opening night of his second-last play, *The Architect*, at the Melbourne Theatre Company. We had already moved into the early stage of me being his occasional carer, and him sometimes

Act One: Love

needing one, and both of us were desperate to remember we were more than that.

I'd always loved the opening nights of Aidan's plays because there was something very sexy about seeing your partner (the man you saw scrubbing the toilet, doing the dishes, cutting his toenails) being celebrated by strangers. It was a night when I would see him in another light. See him as an artist, a thinker, a brain. As the mysterious man with the rolled-up shirt sleeves and the intense eyes drifting through the foyer who had captured my attention all those years before. Not just someone who helped me take the rubbish out and put petrol in the car.

He gripped my knee as we watched the play, his usual way of connecting and sharing the experience. I'd become so accustomed to Aidan's grip on my leg that I could read the code. I whispered that it was *great*. He was *great*. We smiled at each other in the dark as the audience leapt to their feet and applauded for the longest time. There was a standing ovation every night of that season.

To love an artist is to love them for their work and their public persona as well as who they are in private. Or at least that was how I always felt. To see Aidan through the prism of an audience who could sit transfixed for hours by his words and his world was to see him as more than I sometimes did at home.

We left cancer at the door that night. Hit the pause button on his treatment. And chose to forget that it would be the last time we'd share an opening of one his plays.

Scene Three: Ambition

I first laid eyes on Aidan in 1992. He was trying on a vintage overcoat in a church op shop and I watched him through the window as he slipped his arms into the coat's sleeves and modelled it for his friend. His hair was coiffed and black, a little touch of Morrissey. Even from that distance, without ever having spoken, I somehow knew that he and I would grow old together.

At the time, I was living in a share house with university friends. It was a double-storey Edwardian with a cellar we only used for parties. I was trying on being an artist, carrying around second-hand copies of Penguin classics and smoking Winfield Blues and drinking tea in our tiny courtyard from chipped cups we'd stolen from home. I still remember those early days when the drag of smoke spiralled into my lungs. How dizzy it made me. I coughed my way through the first packet, but persevered, smoking on and off in my twenties.

Act One: Love

I was working freelance for a street press, writing articles about artists and interviewing comedians and actors. I'd just finished my bachelor's degree but felt too young to continue studying psychology. Besides, I wanted to be a writer: a journalist with a pen tucked behind my ear, or a lofty novelist with books as thick as weapons. I didn't mind which form my work took; I just wanted to be published.

I'd grown up with bedtime stories of the Australian novelist Peter Carey, who was once married to my aunt – stories of his advertising career that came before his literary success. By the time I was leaving high school in the late eighties, he'd published *Bliss*, *Illywhacker* and *Oscar and Lucinda*. We had copies of them at home and I read these books when I was in my early twenties, thinking perhaps his growing success would rub off on me. After winning the Booker Prize for *Oscar and Lucinda*, he remarried and moved to New York. Even that was romantic in my desperate-to-be-a-writer brain.

I enrolled in a postgraduate degree in professional writing and turned up early to class most weeks, eager to learn. My teacher was a real author with several published books to his name, and I was keen to impress.

He tried it on once, kissing me on a bridge. His body nearing forty made me pull away. I was taken by his mind but not the rest. I'd naively thought we were just friends until he bought me a copy of Georges Bataille's *Story of the Eye*, a 1928 novella about a pair of teenage lovers and their bizarre sexual perversions. Narrated by the male character who is looking back on his life, it is an explicit tale of surrealist erotica. I'd barely begun having sex when he gifted me this, and it both unnerved me and turned me on.

But he scared me too. With his sharp wit and his red pen that would scrawl dispiriting comments on my stories, sending me back to rewrite and rewrite and rewrite. He was the first person to give me genuine feedback. And after years of uncritical and loving responses from my mum, it was a much-needed fall from grace. My stories were *not* brilliant. They needed work. He taught me about rigour and redrafting and how bloody hard it was to be published.

He also taught me about sexual power and that, even though I was considerably younger and desperate for writing success, I didn't feel intimidated saying no.

I discovered he had a reputation. There were stories. Any gender, mostly young, all of us wanting to be writers, appealing, attractive in our vulnerability and our hunger. I stayed away after that and he dropped me from the in-crowd. I was relieved and a little hurt that he could see just how timid I really was. After all, I was born in the seventies and was a teenager in the eighties, a time when women's bodies were both their own and not.

In high school, I'd always believed that I would live somewhere more exotic than my hometown, but when it came to it, leaving Australia like Peter Carey seemed impossible. I was still too tied to my mum and afraid of taking a step that would mean I was truly a grown-up.

Mum always made time to listen to me. Even as I write that, I know it makes me privileged. We had a complex relationship, like many mothers and daughters, but she always made me feel heard. After I left home, she was the one to slip cash into my hand

Act One: Love

and deliver a bag of groceries whenever I saw her. She'd take me shopping for clothes and happily pay as if that was the going rate for an afternoon of my company.

And I'd always return. I'd turn up for the beef lasagne and chocolate mousse in the good martini glasses wide enough to lick the dregs from, turn up for my childhood room and my single bed with my yellow curtains and collection of teddies.

I knew who I wanted to be, but not how to get there. I thought it involved smoking cigarettes, writing poetry and having unsuccessful flings. I dabbled with romance but was afraid of that too.

After I finished university, my dad gifted me an old khaki shirt that Peter Carey used to wear when he was working as a house painter in between jobs. His name is sewn into the collar in red letters on a small cloth label. At the height of my writerly pretension, I wore it when I was banging out my angst-ridden poetry and my short fiction that nobody wanted, pretending that I was channelling his genius.

I still have the shirt tucked away in a drawer.

In my early twenties, when my parents were overseas and I was minding their house, I wrote most of a novel. A sprawling and messy story of family and the traits we inherit without always wanting to. Before email and mobile phones, I would arrange to call Mum at the accommodation she was staying at and read to her. Chapters and chapters of my work. She would offer encouragement from thousands of miles away. The phone bill was huge. It was a time when you paid by the minute and yet she listened.

Every time I wrote a page, a poem, a song, she listened.

I'm embarrassed now about how much I needed her. She read my stories and fixed the spelling. If nobody else was interested, at least she was. She celebrated the tiny wins: the poem published in a literary magazine, the signing with an agent, the unpaid gigs writing reviews of other people's work.

I felt split. I was nearly a woman, living in the inner city, driving a beat-up old car, with a string of semi-successful artist friends, and I was also a girl who would go home to her mum for encouragement and food when things got tough.

Earning about eighty dollars a week in cash, I somehow managed to rent a room and pay for my share of ingredients for our weekly shop. Working for street press meant freebies and a social life that was affordable. I got my name on the door at music venues, tickets to see plays, invites to events that would normally be off limits. The first time Jeff Buckley played in our city, when he sang at the Athenaeum Theatre, I was down the front with my friend's music journalist boyfriend because she was sick, weeping as the strains of 'Hallelujah' lifted us up.

Almost everyone I knew in the mid-nineties was living cheap. None of us had found real jobs except one of my housemates who was working full time at the street press and buying new clothes off the rack. Luckily, she was generous and I had access to her wardrobe. When she bought a short, flowing blue dress for more money than I made in a month, I borrowed it and, whenever I wore it, I felt changed. As if I was suddenly transported to a version of me that might occur sometime in the future. When she later upgraded the dress for something better, she let me keep it and I wore it so often the fabric frayed under my arms and along the seams.

Act One: Love

We spent many nights at a ratty bar where bands played and the pool table was cheap. Most weekends we'd stay late enough to stagger across for hot jam doughnuts at the market as the van pulled up around five am. A bag of six would tide us over until we made it home. My housemate had a crush on one of the band bookers that worked at the bar, and I was just along for the ride. I dated a little back then, but mostly it was the odd pash at a party that went nowhere.

Our sprawling rental house was always full of extras: boyfriends, friends, people passing through. We had an avocado tree in the backyard and one of us would climb onto the roof and bash at the ripest ones while another would try to catch them in a washing basket two floors below. We lived on avocados and sweet potato. None of us could cook. I learnt to make a kidney bean stew that was often on the menu.

Around this time, I successfully pitched some interviews I'd done with comedians to *The Age* and it felt like I was finally growing up. I was being paid per word for these pieces instead of cash slipped in an envelope once a week.

When I landed an interview with Irish comedian Sean Hughes, I knew I'd be able to sell that more broadly. He was already famous and I was already twenty-two. At the time, I wore mid-length tartan skirts, and old kilts I'd found second-hand, with loose-hanging cardigans. My hair was long and straight and trimmed by one of my housemates. I wanted to look bohemian. Instead, I looked eager and clean, like I'd raided my grandma's wardrobe.

I'd grown up watching journalism films: *All the President's Men*, *Broadcast News*, *The China Syndrome*. Holly Hunter as Jane Craig in *Broadcast News* was my pin-up. I too could be tough and hardy, prepared to ask the questions no other young arts journalist would.

I arrived early to the interview, my bag groaning with notebooks and a small tape recorder I'd borrowed from my dad. The interview was over breakfast in a fancy city hotel. Sean Hughes was running late. His publicist found me a seat at a booth and asked me if I wanted a coffee. I asked for a cappuccino, thinking it would be like the ones I'd once drunk in the shopping centre cafeteria with my high-school friends – big white mugs of fluffy air covered in chocolate, the coffee barely strong enough to register.

But this coffee was real and bitter.

When Sean Hughes was introduced to me fifteen minutes later, I'd only managed two small mouthfuls. He sat down and waited. I flicked through my spiral-bound notebook finding the questions I'd written on the tram.

I asked if I could record the interview and he shrugged like he didn't care what I did. I asked my first question. Something insignificant. He answered in one short sentence and I tried another question. And another. But it was clear that I was failing.

He asked me how old I was and what I was hoping to get from the interview. I could sense it was tipping and I wanted it back. He was a big name, pulling decent crowds, and the youngest winner of the Perrier comedy award at the Edinburgh Festival in 1990. This was my scoop.

I told him my ex-boyfriend knew him – thought a connection might help rescue the mess. It didn't. He laughed at me, seeing through my efforts to find common ground.

Embarrassed I back-pedalled, asking different questions,

Act One: Love

channelling Jane Craig from *Broadcast News*. But he started pushing back, wanting to know why I was interviewing him when I clearly didn't know his work. I should have told him that I was being paid fifteen dollars for the article and he hadn't performed in Australia for a year, so how could I know his work? But instead I said nothing.

I couldn't mount a convincing defence and, while my cappuccino cooled, he started on the attack. Ten minutes later, I was crying. He ordered breakfast and I scraped together my things and slid from the booth in my second-hand tartan skirt, desperate to leave.

That day I caught the train home to my parents' house. When I rang Mum from the station, she was surprised. She wasn't expecting me. I made up some story about why I was there when, really, I wanted her to reassure me that I wasn't a fraud.

I didn't sell the piece about Sean Hughes to *The Age*. I had barely enough to cobble together something for street press. And for years after, just hearing his name made me blush.

When I read his obituary in *The Guardian* in 2017, it talked of his ability to find the weakness in someone and pursue it. He must have taken one look at me, trying on sophistication with a coffee I couldn't drink and questions that stunk as immature and childish, and decided I was an easy target.

When I was offered a job reviewing theatre for a new magazine, I took it. Anything to avoid comedians. Theatre seemed less intimidating than comedy. Plus I'd collected programs of all the plays I'd been to when I was younger.

A month after spotting Aidan in the op shop, I went to see a play for work, and there he was again, this time in the foyer surrounded by people. I still didn't know who he was, just that he had hair that looked important, and a way of moving that said he was much more comfortable in the arts world than me.

I was with Mum who had made identifying famous people in the wild an artform. I'd be mid-sentence and she'd fling her head around after catching a glimpse of someone from a show she could never quite remember. As a twenty-something desperate to work as an artist, it always embarrassed me. I preferred pretending they meant nothing and had mastered the blank look brilliantly.

That night, I was once again wearing a tartan skirt and had my hair in some elaborate plait. Aidan didn't notice me in the crowd, but I took the sighting as a sign, confident that at some point our lives would intersect. I just had to be ready.

Several months passed and a friend called me to see if I'd like to do publicity for a theatre company that he ran with two others. Like much of the work I did back then, it was unpaid. Naturally, I said yes.

On my first day, I turned up to a meeting of ten or so theatre folk who all knew each other from university. I was the outsider. A little overwhelmed by the shared humour, stories and confidence, I was quieter than usual. When Aidan walked in and took his seat at the end of the table as the third member of the company, I didn't know where to look. I was so close I could have reached out and touched his arm.

There are photographs from this time of me looking on, not quite in the group, but hovering close to the edges, eager to be invited in. They look like the cast of *The Breakfast Club* bonded at the end of the movie, and I'm one of the extras at the beginning, clearly not bad enough to be in detention after all.

Act One: Love

I was dogged in my pursuit of Aidan. And if I'm honest, it wasn't my first rodeo. I'd pursued love interests before and not always honourably. There was a hippie boy who hung out at the same bar I did, who I ended up dating for twenty-four hours, and an engineering student at university who dumped me, so I dated his identical twin for revenge. There were always potential romances but most of them fizzled out fast without making an impact. Aidan was different. He was smart, funny, a writer of plays, with great hair and impeccable style and living in an edgy flat in St Kilda. I couldn't stop wanting him, even though he didn't seem to feel the same.

Sometimes I'd drive past his flat pretending it was on my way home. Later, one of his friends would comment on my car, having noticed it zipping past his place more than once when she was over having a wine. We laughed about it, but I had to admit that I was always watching when I drove down his street, just in case he was on his balcony and he waved me inside.

Looking back, I'm not sure what I was doing. There was a sort of misguided desperation about it all. Friends were embarrassed on my behalf and tried to stage various interventions, pointing out all the reasons that it was never going to happen, but I just couldn't let it be.

At some point in the next four years, Aidan and I became friends. Solid, close and remarkable friends who told each other things. He was always in relationships with glamorous actors who seemed so much more than me. And I was always in disastrous flirtations, not really investing because by then I was completely in love with him.

Then, on the night of my twenty-sixth birthday, our friend held a party for me in her warehouse in Easey Street in Collingwood. We cooked a thrifty feast for thirty, and Aidan turned up. He was sullen and moody because he'd just broken up with his girlfriend of five years. We drank too much and caught a cab back to St Kilda, where we both lived. I said goodnight, went inside to the little flat that I shared with my friend and he went home. Then he called me minutes later from his landline. Said he'd be over soon.

That was when it started. That night. Messy and complicated but somehow right. At first, we kept things secret, telling only his flatmate when I stayed over. Mostly though, we pretended we weren't together, that we were just friends. Now I'm not sure why. Maybe neither of us thought it would last. Or at least maybe Aidan didn't.

It was the early days of mobile phones and I had one before he did. A Nokia flip-phone that my son now covets for its retro coolness. Aidan's calls to me would be from his landline. Later, he used to text me cute messages, but back then it was just hours spent racking up expensive phone bills.

Nine months after my birthday dinner, I was living in a noisy share house on Nicholson Street when I agreed to move in with him. Neither of us had ever shared our space so intimately before and suddenly we were opening joint bank accounts and trying to budget, living on artists' wages and dreaming big.

My friend helped me move my carload of stuff into Aidan's because he was away on tour with a play. We drove across the river from our rented house in North Fitzroy to Aidan's rented flat opposite St Kilda Botanical Gardens and lugged boxes up the two flights of stairs.

Act One: Love

I remember us giggling about me moving in. It suddenly seemed so ridiculous, so grown-up, so unreal. I think she was the first to notice that there was no television set. We walked back downstairs, climbed into her car and drove to a whitegoods store. Of course, I had no money. In those days I was living week-to-week. The salesperson offered me a television on a finance scheme that would see me pay four times its worth over the next two years. But I was twenty-six and I didn't care about such things as small print, so I signed my name, lugged the giant box out to my friend's car and giggled some more as we struggled to carry it into the flat.

Aidan had lived there for years. Owned by some guy at the pub on the corner, it was cheap. With a view of the park, a sixties balcony that stretched across its face and original parquetry floors, it was too grand for me. I was used to slumming it in the smallest bedroom in a share house, not shacking up with my partner in a flat that could have been featured in a magazine spread.

I remember that night when my friend left: how she hugged me and said something about how Aidan would have beautiful silver hair in years to come. I think she meant when he was the age of his dad.

He didn't grow old, but his hair did turn silver and then eventually white. I still think of that comment often. How in our twenty-six-year-old minds, my friend and I saw moving in together as the beginning of a lifelong partnership, assuming Aidan and I would grow old together, never considering the possibility that something would derail that.

After my friend left, I sat on Aidan's couch with my new television, on the other side of the river, wondering what I had just done.

Scene Four: Bowerbirds

Our children often complain about having writers for parents, joking that nothing they do is safe from being used for material. I admit that I haven't taken those complaints very seriously because, up until now, Aidan and I both mostly wrote fiction. But this book changes that. I know here that the line is blurred between being a parent and being a writer, and I'm aware that I want to be a parent first.

As I finish each chapter, my children search for themselves on the page, checking they are comfortable with how they have been presented. Sometimes our conversations swerve into discussions of memory, as we have vastly different recollections of the same moment in time. Things Aidan might have said, events of a holiday, clothes he wore, intentions made, are suddenly all up for grabs. The process of defending our own version is often heated and outspoken and, still, we circle three separate versions, adamant that ours is the *right* one.

Act One: Love

Some nights, as our family dinners become family dissections, I find myself feeling uneasy about what I thought was true. Nowhere is this more apparent than in how we recollect our childhood and how we make sense of those adult moments through the lens of a child.

Listening to observations made by the kids about their parents makes me reconsider arguments between Aidan and me – what we both believed was being said, how we catalogued those words for another day and fired them later like hard little bullets. Perhaps when we came to retrieve those bullets, they were not accurate memories at all, but a sort of emotional mash-up.

Aidan was fascinated by the concept of brain elasticity and in 2013 wrote a play called *The House on the Lake* in which the main character had anterograde amnesia, a type of memory loss preventing the formation of new memories. It was a thriller, a two-hander, where a forensic psychologist interviews the main character about the alleged murders of his wife and her lover. The psychologist must ascertain whether the amnesia is real or fabricated as a defence, suspecting that the man is responsible for the murders and is playing the memory-loss card as a way out.

In a folder on Aidan's computer, I found some of his musings about the play explaining his interest in memory. He talks about *theatre being the perfect platform in which to examine the binary oppositions of truth and lying. The great paradox of theatre is that it is a tightly constructed lie designed to reveal truth. It's an elaborate con.*

In talking about the play, he links truth and memory, but I

suspect that is where we are undone. There is no one truth in memory – just an attempt at such.

I remember learning about state-dependent memory when I studied psychology at university: the concept that a person will be more likely to accurately retrieve memories if they are in the same state they were in when they first encoded the information. The example our lecturer gave was of a study that showed if you learnt a foreign language while drunk, you had a better chance at recalling it if you were in the same state, rather than if you were sober.

Of course, we all ran to the pub to try it out.

French author Marcel Proust coined the phrase 'involuntary memory' in his seven-volume novel, *À la recherche du temps perdu* or *In Search of Lost Time*. The novel explores the idea that a particular smell can suddenly transport us involuntarily to a particular time. Proust's example was that when he ate the French cake madeleine, he was instantly returned to his childhood.

A very stinky early memory I have is of the pickled onions my grandmother made when I was young. An old-fashioned recipe, she steeped small white onions in brown vinegar, sugar, cloves and other spices. She used to cook them in her one-room flat in the public housing tower overlooking Williamstown Bay and divvy up the jars among the family.

A vinegar smell snaps me back to when I was holding a slippery onion between my fingers and I was biting at the layers, tearing each one away with my teeth, before moving on to the next. I would work my way through an entire jar unless a parent took it away.

Act One: Love

It is not only the onions I remember now when I smell vinegar, but also a series of snapshots of my gran. I remember that she was happiest when sitting under a tree, with her portable silver ashtray and a half-eaten neenish tart, and that she always carried an opened bag of Jersey Caramels in her pocket. Once, on the hunt for these sweets, I slid my fingers into her dressing-gown pocket and they collided with an open pair of sharp nail scissors that took off the top of my finger and meant a trip to the doctor for stitches.

Distinctive smells can take me leapfrogging through my past from one moment to the next. During lockdown, a friend dropped off a small bottle of Chanel No. 5 with a note that read: *All the strong women in my life have worn this scent, and when I wear it, I find it helps.* With one spray on my wrist, I was back in my mum's bedroom, watching her dress. I could follow the trail of her scent through the house, along the slate floors, down the corridor, to the kitchen.

And there she was.

Cooking.

Mum was a magician in the kitchen, born from the frugal meals of her childhood when a single mother's income was not enough to buy groceries. She never wore an apron, never used a peeler and rarely bothered with recipes. She was self-taught and unafraid.

Dinner parties meant watching Mum experiment. She prepared Lebanese *kibbeh*, rolling the oblong shapes in her hands before gently frying them. She made zabaglione ice cream and froze it in fancy thick-stemmed clear glasses, one for each guest. There were stuffed peppers, rich chocolate mousse and homemade tortellini from a recipe taught to her by one of her dearest friends. She cooked for acknowledgement, liking the praise. I fear she spent much of those early years, raising children and stuck at home out in the sticks, missing her life in the city. Food was her way of clawing it back.

My brother and I always went hunting in the mornings after these dinners. We'd scrape out the last few crusty mouthfuls of chocolate mousse or finish off a square of pumpernickel bread with some hours-old dip smeared onto it. But the real treasure was intact After Dinner Mints still in their slips of black paper. Those were too good to share.

Some weekends, I would go yabbying in the neighbour's dam, wade in with my homemade nets and catch as many yabbies as I could to bring home for lunch. Mum would toss them into boiling water and then it was my turn to peel their skins and pull the poo pipe out. I can still feel the crusted shell cracking under my fingernails and taste the sweet white meat fried quickly in a head of garlic and salted butter. Mum and I would eat them from the pan. A fork in each hand, we'd shovel them in, pleased the boys in the house didn't like them too.

Now I fry spicy marinated prawns for my daughter and we sit the heavy enamel frypan on a wooden board between us and eat the lot, the smell of spices reminding me of the many times we've eaten like this.

When Aidan was alive, family dinners were sacred times of the day. The four of us would gather at the table and talk, sometimes play cards while we ate or hold a music quiz. If Aidan had cooked then the meal would be pasta or schnitzel, homemade pizza or tacos – meals that were simple and loved by the kids. It was Aidan who taught me how to make stock from the end of the roast chicken, never wasting the scraps of meat that would go into a soup for dinner the next day.

He introduced the kids to the delight of stopping off on a road trip for a beef pie and sauce at a country bakery. I would always order a salad roll with extra beetroot and raw white onion, but the three of them would devour their pies and then rate them. Sometimes the pastry was too soggy, other times the meat too chunky and, on occasion, the pie was so good they went back for seconds. Now when we drive past a bakery in a small town, I find myself stopping so the kids can buy their pies and remember their dad.

We hunt Aidan out where we can, but find him in different ways. When my son and I holidayed in Japan for two weeks, we visited many of the places we'd been years earlier as a family. My memory wasn't sharp like his; he's inherited his father's way of locating himself in place, using visual cues to find where he is. When he led me on a search for a giant crab that he'd photographed with Aidan eight years before in an Osaka alleyway, I told him that I doubted he would find it, wanting to prevent disappointment.

I followed as he pushed through crowds on a steamy summer's night in the weaving backstreets of Namba and stopped outside the seafood place where a fading orange crab is suspended overhead. He snapped off a photograph on his phone before grinning at me, as if to say: *See, I was right.*

Travelling to a place you have only seen once before with the person you now miss is a tormenting experience. You keep waiting for them to point out a funny sign or stop at that market stall to try a food they like. You even buy the same doughnuts from the same shop they did, hoping to taste connection.

Returning to Japan meant re-accessing all of those memories from when Aidan was there too. He was like a ghost tourist, a vague shape at our shoulders, and we both felt him as we drifted through familiar landscapes, sampling foods we first ate with him, and then leaving him behind as we sought out the new.

When I was a child, all I wanted was the sort of photographic memory I'd seen in films. This was partly to do with the fact that my younger brother's memory was always more impressive than mine and our parents often deferred to his version of events because they believed there was a fair chance that he had it right. I wish I knew then what I know now about how memory works. I may have been able to cast doubt over his adamant recollections of our childhood and painted him as a much more unreliable narrator.

Even now, at extended family dinners, his memory is held up as the *true* one. He is the reporter of facts, whereas I am the storyteller, the constructor of narratives more dramatic than truth. I have long accepted this, deferring to his versions, largely because half the time I can't remember anything. Grief, perhaps, has shaped my thoughts, squashed childhood memories into tiny gaps, making room for more important things like that first time I saw Aidan through the op-shop window. Or maybe it's brain fog, that casually mentioned condition that afflicts women of my age. Whatever it is, I sometimes start a book, read one hundred pages or so before I start to question if I've read it before. My memory is no longer solid and dependable.

Nowhere are memories more desperately hunted for than when someone dies. A time when grief makes even the smallest thought often impossible and when we are bumbling through guilt and hurt and longing. Surely during such heightened emotion, memories have no chance at being accurate?

Once, we considered memory to be something that was stored like a film in the brain that we could return to and retrieve at will, but now we understand that memories are not a permanent record of what happened. They are constructed and many things can impact on and alter their construction. Researchers today believe memory is written in the synapses in the brain, the places where neurons connect. And as these connections are used, they can become stronger which then encodes the memory. Canadian neuroscientist Sheena Josselyn has written about mistaken memories possibly being caused by the inclusion of some neurons and the exclusion of others from the physical storage of memory.

How memories are retrieved is constantly being debated. Some researchers believe that once a memory is constructed, it is consolidated – that is, it may fade, but it is relatively stable each time it is returned to. Other researchers believe there is scope for memories to be reconsolidated each time they are recalled, so they can be altered or disrupted by the recall process. And in France, neuroscientists have successfully implanted false memories into mice.

This may sound like something from a science fiction novel, but American psychologist Elizabeth Loftus believes that false memories can be implanted without technology, simply by the language we use to describe a memory: those words can change the way we remember it. She argues that suggestive questioning of eyewitness testimony can distort recollections and create false memories, particularly when people of colour are the accused. Her research into false memory is underpinned by her belief that humans do not have a permanent capacity for memory because memories are reconstructed and not replayed.

The idea that we can inflate our memories, alter them, distort them or even create false ones, is overwhelming to someone grieving. I am not a clinical psychologist, but I do have an interest in the mechanics of memory. I like imagining that what I remember about Aidan is real and true. I want to hold on to those memories, return to them at will and argue for their existence.

But I also understand that my version of events is not the only one and that if I asked my children about their memories of the day Aidan died, theirs would be different from mine.

If I close my eyes and try to see that day, the cat is curled under his bed, the vial of morphine is cool in my hand, his breathing is laboured, the sun is warm through the glass, the words of the nurse are distant before she leaves. Sensory scraps build to construct the scene in the same way Aidan would have considered the ending of a play.

But I know I can't remember Aidan's face in those last seconds, or who I hugged first afterwards, or even what was said.

As writers we are stealers of other people's memories, bowerbirds of story. Sometimes we use our own memories as material – even when we are writing fiction – conversations we've had with friends, lovers we've known, a night sitting under a Moreton Bay fig tree back at the beginning of something. But it might just as easily be a memory that belongs to someone else.

Aidan used family memories in his plays. *The Gap* was produced not long after I first met him. It was inspired by the death of his second cousin, Tony Stewart, one of the Balibo Five. Tony, a sound recordist, was the youngest of a group of journalists killed during the Indonesian incursions in East Timor in 1975. Aidan wrote the play based on the deaths of the men and of the political dance by our government to secure an oil deal in the Timor Sea. *The Gap* was a heightened play, less about Tony and more about grubby political handshaking. Aidan found a way to touch on the personal while using theatrical devices to broaden the story.

In 2010, he wrote a new play about the Balibo Five. *National Interest* opened at Melbourne Theatre Company in 2012. In it, he examined a character based on his Aunt June and the grief she felt at losing Tony in East Timor.

> JUNE: At first, I was consumed. I ate my grief. Dined on it. But with time I learnt to take it out of myself. And now it sits beside me. Always.

The play was haunting, devastating and more personal than the previous work. Aidan worried that by writing it, he'd trampled on the family legacy of Tony's death. He worried his cousins would be offended, hurt by his theatricalised story.

It didn't belong to Aidan. But it preoccupied him. It was one painful part of his family narrative.

As writers we defend our position, our right to tell a story because it is what we do. But it's a flimsy disguise, one that collapses when met with the hurt of those we write about. And nowhere is that more apparent than when writing non-fiction and the writer is the protagonist. It is hard to remove the writer part of me from the parent part, the friend part, the partner part or the child part. To write my version of the truth, my memories, I must also think about how my words will impact on all the people in my life – not just on me.

How do we approach the notion of truth, of our story, when it is never only ours to tell?

When Aidan died, my version of the story lost its challenger and my memories of us became mine alone. He cannot flesh out the anecdote about the bar in East London where we drank homemade vodka and danced until dawn, or remind me of the time our daughter said her first word when she yelled 'Mama' from her portable cot on a weekend away, or laugh at the botched speech we made together on stage when we won an award for our short film. I must try to hold on to these moments without him to prompt and nudge and correct.

Our children are now holders of our collective family memory too. And their personal truth is often very different from mine. I remember Aidan teaching them to ride bikes, taking them fishing off the pier, going on date days with one at a time and crying in films, showing them how to enjoy a Vegemite and butter sandwich on square white bread. I remember him debating philosophy, showing them the stars and dancing in the loungeroom with the music up too loud.

I see him in them. In the way they move through the world.

Act One: Love

But their memories are not mine. Their memories are theirs. Perhaps if the three of us each keep sharing our memories, then we can cobble together a sort of patchwork of moments to keep Aidan present.

Scene Five: Soundtrack

If someone wants to know me, they can read the books on my shelves. There, they will learn about the mechanics of my taste, find clues to pages I stopped at where I've bent corners for later, like in Shirley Hazzard's *The Transit of Venus*, see multiple editions of Carson McCullers's *The Heart Is a Lonely Hunter* and follow my journey from Plath poetry to grisly crime.

To know Aidan, you could listen to his soundtrack, the songs he returned to, the tracks that filled his days.

When we were first dating, he would sing to me on road trips: '(Up a) Lazy River' by The Mills Brothers, Cab Calloway's 'St James Infirmary Blues', and a song he wrote about staring out at the slate grey sea that our dear friend sang at his memorial. I never realised at the time how much music flavoured his days, kept his heart beating. I thought when he sang to me that he was just being romantic.

Act One: Love

Aidan played self-taught guitar and sang with a rich, melodic voice. He messed around with lyrics and tunes but couldn't read music. He'd grown up with the voices of Jim Croce and The Ink Spots and still played them sometimes, reminiscing about his dad's love for those bands.

We'd go and see live music together: Teenage Fanclub, The Lemonheads, Saint Etienne. We had different tastes. I liked folky female voices singing about love and troubles. He liked blokes with smart lyrics telling stories with big guitars. He introduced me to albums I'd never heard, to singers dead before my time and to the way that songs stain your memories, giving them meaning they don't have in silence.

Even now, if I hear Lou Reed's 'Perfect Day' or Turin Brakes's 'Future Boy', I'm back in 2001 on a train travelling across Europe with Aidan, each of us wearing one earphone to listen to the mixed CD that our friend burnt us before we left.

In the years we lived together, our house was rarely quiet. Music was as much a measure of the day as meals were. Dreamy jazz in the mornings, something light and modern through the day and then, as we wandered in for dinner, he'd choose the perfect 'eating music'. At bedtime, he'd sing the kids to sleep with a Willie Nelson track like 'Stardust' or 'Moonlight in Vermont'. Mostly he cared only for songs with lyrics because, to him, storytelling was everything.

When he died, we missed his noise and hunted out the songs that gave rhythm to his life. We played albums that he loved, some worming their way into our hearts more than others. The Tim Rogers & the Twin Set album *What Rhymes with Cars and*

Girls was a favourite of Aidan's. Our daughter learnt the songs on guitar and sang along as she played, the lyrics bleeding into the spaces where Aidan no longer was. Aidan used to plug his phone into the cigarette lighter in the car so he could play the album through the stereo that was as old as our son. He thought Tim was a beautiful lyricist.

That album was released in 1999 not long after Aidan and I had just started living together. It was a time when we were dreaming up stories, hosting dinners with friends and nesting. When Aidan wrote a play titled *What Rhymes with Cars and Girls* based on the album many years later, I didn't realise that it would come to represent so much of who we were. The story of settling down, falling in love, surrendering, hoping. The story of fucking up and coming back together. He wrote the play to accompany the songs, describing it in a synopsis he wrote as *a love story. It's about the miraculous ease of falling in love and the difficulty of holding on to it.*

His plays were always about relationships, but *What Rhymes with Cars and Girls* is the only one that tackles romantic intimacy. It is like a conversation between lovers as they try to navigate the trickiness of love.

I choose to see the play as an ode to us in many ways. There were scenes lifted from the first road trip we ever took as a freshly minted couple, driving up the coast to meet Aidan's new literary agent, and a night we spent with five dollars in our bank accounts with a long neck of beer, just sitting under a giant Moreton Bay fig tree on the harbour, telling stories aflush with love.

Perhaps this is why I return to this play so often now, searching for clues about our past, about how he felt about me. This scene where Johnno notices an old couple in the park always spoke to me.

Act One: Love

JOHNNO: Just then I stop.
I grab Tash by the hand.
We're walking through a park and there just ahead of us …
Passing under one of the old lamps …
Is a couple …
An old couple walking slowly …
Hand in hand.
You can see the old fella's bent over like a twig and she's dressed up to the nines …
Got her hair up.

TASH: She's laughing at something he's said.

JOHNNO: And you can see him chuckling too on his bent frame …
At the pleasure he's just given her …
And just like that they pass through the light and …
They are gone.

TASH: … Took my breath away.

JOHNNO: … It was like seeing a path …
One that goes on forever … right in front of us.
And like a big sook I just started crying.
Right there in the park.
Never forget it …

A year or so after Aidan died, a friend mounted a student production of the play at the school where she worked. We drove out to watch it on a freezing Saturday night, sitting together under layers of blankets we lugged with us from home. The audience seats were one and a half metres apart because of social distancing, but I could still hear my son unwrapping his Chupa Chups in the dark.

The cast were two year-twelve students, and the line-up of musicians and teachers at the school. It wasn't polished like the Melbourne Theatre Company production had been, but it was full of the same heart and the same magic.

As the character of Johnno spoke about his tank of tropical fish, the kids both looked down the line of the seats at me, recognising the reference to our aquatic pets and understanding that their dad had woven details of their lives into his play.

When an artist dies, there is a body of work that remains. A way of connecting to the person you love. But a play is not like other forms of art. It is a living thing, created to be performed. There is no way to revisit it once the production ends. Then a play begins its long hibernation, waiting for another company to stage it. No two seasons will be the same. Each one will have a different director, cast, designer, theatre. It will never be the work you first saw.

In an interview Aidan did with Melbourne Theatre Company back in 2017, he said: *A play isn't very much of a thing without a production and an audience. It's a set of instructions, like a manual for a car. But what's a car unless it's driven? And then what use is the manual?*

To see his play performed again felt like a gift. Watching the

Act One: Love

student production, with young actors testing their talent in a freezing gym hall on the outskirts of regional Victoria, made me realise that it didn't matter who said Aidan's words, they were recognisably his. Expressions he'd use, slang, jokes he'd tell in the house.

As we drove home that night, in the darkness of a country freeway, we listened to the album. The three of us were quiet as we heard the lyrics and the melody afresh, like it was a trail of breadcrumbs leading us to understanding Aidan in a different way.

When Tim Rogers & the Twin Set recently reformed to release a new album after twenty-three years, I rushed out and bought it. For Aidan. The album is a companion piece. A sequel. A mellowing. A follow-up. Like we are re-meeting the same characters twenty-three years later, when they have had children, lost parents and started going to the odd AA meeting.

It could have been written for us.

Called *Tines of Stars Unfurled*, all the songs on this album refer to songs on *What Rhymes with Cars and Girls*, like a conversation across time.

At first, I found it jarring, listening alone, like the world had moved on without Aidan. Like the album he loved had all grown up and left him behind. But then my daughter and I saw the band perform the songs live in the same venue where we had farewelled Aidan at his memorial and something clicked.

I listened to the lyrics differently that night. I heard lines I knew Aidan would have smiled at – stories painted that would have moved him. I tried to listen as he would have, and the songs opened up, curled their way around me and returned me to a time when he was still here.

I play this album when I'm driving in my car now. And it feels like Aidan is beside me, listening along, singing a little, pointing out a phrase he thinks I've missed and laughing when I butcher the lyrics as I sing, out of tune and time.

Scene Six:
Family

Aidan was the youngest of ten. Another child was born after him, but he died before taking his first breaths and so Aidan claimed his place as the baby of the family.

When I met him, he already had a swarm of nephews and nieces. He didn't always remember all their names. There were just so many of them.

Where my family was neat, compact and close, his was large, loud and sprawling. At the beginning, I bumbled through conversations with a bunch of men who all looked the same. Dark-haired, fair-skinned and with eyebrows the size of caterpillars, I struggled to tell one from the next. When we saw them, I'd feel overwhelmed by their shared humour and their anecdotes. Not in an unpleasant way, just in an unfamiliar one.

His mother was a fierce matriarch. Small and grey-haired, she smoked, wore scarlet lipstick and read dense crime novels borrowed from the library. Once she gifted me a kilo of cheese and I'm still not sure why. She dubbed the partners of her children 'The Outlaws'. His father was gentle, a knitter, who called me 'Bossa Nova', later shortening it to 'Bossy'.

Back then, we were the only unmarried couple without children in the family. We didn't own a house, our car was barely going, and we were always gambling that the next project would be *the* one.

Not long after we started living together, one of Aidan's brothers was hospitalised in Bendigo with a resistant form of pneumococcal. The family descended on the town and I watched as each member met the challenge of illness and adopted a role. One dug for medical information. Another kept watch over the oldies. One even arrived in their decked-out Kombi called 'Arabella' and he and his wife set up a temporary kitchen outside the hospital, serving coffee and toasted sandwiches to anyone in need. It was like an army of look-alike soldiers sweeping in and erecting temporary barracks to protect one of their own.

A black humour settled over us. The first night everyone decamped to the local university accommodation and stayed in student rooms, drinking cheap sherry and white wine after dinner. I left the next day, went home to our flat and waited for the phone call. A family of lapsed and practising Catholics, they knew how to stage a vigil. Whispered prayers, shared memories and a million cups of undrunk tea were their company as they waited.

I returned when it was clear that he wasn't going to make it. His eldest son, only just an adult himself, punched a hole in the wall of the hospital kitchen as the tension of the waiting dragged everyone under. I didn't visit his bedside, feeling more like an

Act One: Love

outsider rather than a confirmed family member. Instead, I tried to be helpful in the waiting room, rubbing backs, holding hands and keeping the kettle filled with water.

The funeral for Aidan's brother was messy and sad. He was forty-seven when he died and everyone was hurting. The soundtrack was a loud mix of Irish music and Aussie rock as they sat around late into the night telling stories and drinking. One of Aidan's sisters spoke about a bird that had visited her that she sensed was a reincarnation of her brother. I remembered that conversation years later when my mother died and a fat grey pigeon began visiting us each afternoon. Mum would have hated being thought of as that bird, but I found it comforting as it hopped across the uneven brickwork to watch my son hang upside-down on his climbing frame after he'd just perfected a trick.

The lessons in crisis management I learnt from Aidan's family came in handy later in my life when I would act as a sort of gatekeeper for my own hospital vigils. But until that week in Bendigo, I'd never been close to death before. My grandparents had died when I was overseas travelling and I didn't make it back for their funerals. I'd never had pets as a child, so I hadn't discovered how to mourn.

But death was understood by Aidan. His childhood animals had died, his grandparents, the baby next in line to him. But the point when grief wired its way into his DNA was when his sister died back in 1989, three years before I first met him. She was deeply loved and her loss was acute. Aidan used to say that when he was a young child, he thought she was his mother because there were so many children that he couldn't work out who he belonged to.

My childhood was safe and cocooned and nothing like that of the seventies upbringing many of my friends had. Where Mum had grown up without anyone watching, she was determined to smother my brother and me with whatever we needed. She gave up her career to stay home and raise us. There was just the four of us. Dad working long hours and commuting to the city and Mum always hovering in the frame.

Aidan's childhood was different from mine. With so many children and cousins nearby, his house was full. He shared a room, whereas I had my own. He wore hand-me-downs, while Mum sewed most of my clothes herself. His parents were busy and overwhelmed by the sheer number of people in the house. Later, when we had children, Aidan couldn't remember a story being read to him at bedtime and he marvelled at my patience in reading the same books again and again to our kids, just as my mum had done all those years before.

Two years after his brother died in Bendigo, Aidan's eldest brother died of a brain tumour. As sharply funny as Aidan, I had only just started properly getting to know him. It rocked Aidan to lose his eldest sibling. He was smart and quick-witted and had the same salt-and-pepper hair that Aidan would grow into after our daughter was born.

This death was also fast. Untreatable, unpreventable and unbelievable. The family was shrinking. Aidan's ageing parents had buried three adult children and they seemed lost with loss.

Act One: Love

Then another brother went to hospital. When we visited him, he was still in control of the room. It was the dominant feature that ran through the family – this dark, underhanded wit that could totally disarm and charm and make it impossible to feel anything but fondness. His family was intoxicating to me. They had their own code, their own references that I didn't understand. It was like a Russian novel that I couldn't get enough of.

Over the following years, Aidan farewelled that next brother, his niece and both his parents. He became skilled at saying goodbye. It was a brutal time. There were jokes about meeting up at the next funeral. At his father's, Aidan gave one of the eulogies for the family and then went immediately to the opening night of the play he was directing at the Melbourne Theatre Company and delivered the main address. There was no time to grieve. No time to stop. Three of his big productions for Melbourne Theatre Company each began their lives with a loss of one of his family.

The Christmas gathering after Aidan's brother died in Bendigo in 2003 was held in our backyard. Fifty people squashed into the scrappy space around the large gum tree that had been planted many years before by a woman who'd knocked on our front door one day to see if it was still there. And cried when she saw it was.

I was pregnant with our first child but not telling anyone yet. Aidan had borrowed a giant metal spit to roast the pig we'd bought to feed his family. I remember one of the many small children found the pig rotating in the shed and reported back about it looking dead.

Our daughter was born five months before Aidan's eldest brother died. And then we had our son three years later. Having these bursts of life and energy and joy, among so much sadness, perhaps saved Aidan at the time and gave him a messy, noisy, sleepless house to retreat to.

But in many ways it didn't seem real. And Aidan seemed okay. Like he was coping. Like he could deal with all this death. Until my mum was diagnosed with cancer in 2010 and I went from supporting Aidan to dropping everything and caring for her.

She was overseas when she first developed symptoms. On the trip of a lifetime, walking through villages in Spain, her breathing became sticky. She bought a Ventolin pump from the chemist, deciding it was just asthma. She'd never had asthma before, but she'd been plagued by lung problems all her life. Pleurisy, pneumonia, a collapsed lung. My childhood was peppered with visits to hospitals to see her.

Twenty months later, Mum died from adenocarcinoma, a type of lung cancer that begins in mucus-producing cells and accounts for about forty per cent of all lung cancers. It is common in smokers but also the most common lung cancer in people who've never smoked. For much of this time, she couldn't breathe properly. She would lie with pillows strategically placed under her back and undergo excruciatingly painful operations to remove the fluid in her lungs.

Our children were eight and four and Aidan was working a hundred hours a week at Melbourne Theatre Company, or so it felt, and Mum needed me.

I juggled parenting with caring for Mum and drove across the Yarra River from Brunswick in the north to Elwood in the south more times than I can remember. Even now, crossing the Hoddle Bridge at certain times of the day, I'm back in a sort of sad mist that followed me during those days.

Act One: Love

When she moved to palliative care two weeks before she died, her lungs had refilled with fluid. She was so weak that I had to hold the oxygen mask to her face, helping her along. Her words paled as the air left her and by the end she weighed almost nothing. When the death rattle came, it was a whimper, soft and small.

Afterwards I breathed. Full, rich breaths. Like I was dispelling all the fears I held for her and breathing enough air for us both.

The night of Mum's funeral, Aidan apologised to me that he couldn't be more present for my grief. He tried to explain that the tone of the winter light affected him because his sister had died at that same time of year. He believed you stored grief in your body and it returned when the environment was right.

Then he told me, 'I'm done with death.'

At the time it stung that he was so cavalier with my loss. But now that he's gone too and my grief has leaked out onto everything, I understand what he meant. There's a limit to how much you can feel. And to how many treasured people you can farewell without being changed.

Aidan might have been done with death but, of course, death is never done with anyone.

Scene Seven:
Memento Mori

Memento mori is a Latin phrase meaning 'remember you must die'. The phrase was well used in medieval times when people believed that life on earth was preparation for the afterlife. Artists have represented the stoic philosophy through skull art, rotting fruit, watches, hourglasses – anything that portrays the fleeting nature of life.

One of my favourite depictions of *memento mori* is Vincent van Gogh's painting *Skull of a Skeleton with Burning Cigarette* from 1885–86. In it, a skeleton is smoking a lit cigarette, and many believe it was painted as a satirical statement born out of boredom at the classes he was undertaking. But van Gogh's father had recently died and his own health was bad at the time, with rotting teeth and stomach complaints, so perhaps he was also responding to his mortality. He died five years later after shooting himself in the chest.

Act One: Love

Despite the fact the skeleton is a skeleton, it appears to be posing for a portrait, smoking like van Gogh did in the day.

I like this painting because it's playful and death so rarely is. I also like this painting because it reminds me of Aidan and the way he smoked when we first lived together.

It feels almost illicit writing about cigarettes and smoking now, but in the early to mid-nineties most people I knew smoked. We smoked for affect, we smoked to fill the time, we smoked because we were addicted.

Aidan was a smoker way back when I first met him. Like most artists in their twenties living in share houses and not thinking about the future, he smoked Peter Stuyvesant soft pack. He stopped in his thirties, became healthier when we had children and stayed that way until he had a breakdown in 2015.

That happened when he was staying in another city, having flown there for the last week of rehearsals for his new play. It was his second production in a matter of months. His other production had just finished its season and had been a notable success.

He rang me from the hotel. Told me I needed to fly up earlier than we'd planned for the opening night. He said he couldn't leave the hotel room. That something had happened and he didn't know what it was. He sounded terrified on the phone. I rang my dad. He took the kids and I jumped on a plane, unsure of what I'd find.

The hotel room stank of cigarettes and cheap white wine. He was in bed, incapable of leaving. I didn't know what to do. He was shaky and scared but couldn't tell me what was wrong.

I made him shower. I made him come for a walk around the block, stopping to buy supplies from the supermarket that I thought he could manage to keep down: bananas and bread and packets of chips.

We made it to the opening night of the play. He was tense and silent. We left as soon as the second curtain call ended. And the next day we flew home where he immediately went back to bed. And there he stayed for months and months. Crying and not eating. He couldn't make it through a meal without tears rolling down his face. We found a psychologist who started unpacking years of neglected grief. As his depression grew, he started drinking too much.

After a while I started escaping with the kids. We'd head out of town for weekends. I didn't know what else to do. The sicker Aidan became the more withdrawn he was and the harder it grew to reach him. I was trying to earn money with school author visits and teaching while trying to shield the kids from the worst of him. He was a shell of sadness and tears, and the longer it went on, the more he drank.

After six months, I rang his best friends – three excellent women who had been in his life forever. They took him in, moving him between their houses, so that the kids and I could have a break. This was around the time I took out private health insurance to see if I could wrangle him into a private clinic so that he could get intensive mental-health help and dry out.

We went to an appointment with a psychiatrist who would assess his readiness for admittance into a clinic. He sat next to me in her consultation room, smelling like cigarettes. He'd lost twenty kilos over the past six months and was looking more like he did when I'd first met him way back when. But his mind was still the sharpest it had ever been. As she asked questions, he answered with brutal honesty: 'No, there's no point going into the clinic because there's no hope. I have no hope.'

Later, he started writing a book about this time. I didn't read it then, but I've read it since. It is us. Him and me. I am she.

> She waved him away with her hand and moved off some distance, nodding and speaking quietly. He stood, like an old dog at the rear entrance to the clinic. To his left there was a long glass window. A grizzled man stood there watching him. He mouthed the words 'fuck off' before realising it was his own reflection he was talking to. Looking at himself, he straightened up, sucked in his gut, and took off his hat. There seemed to be little or no improvement to the ghostly reflection. In fact, it seemed worse. A ratty mane of grey hair shot up from his head, lips held tight, a hard face.
> When did all this happen, he thought. He was only 49.

In the book that he was writing, the couple visit a therapist and have a conversation almost identical to the one Aidan and I had with the psychiatrist. Even in his fiction, I sometimes spoke for him, if it is me performing the role of Beth in the scene. The story continues:

> 'So, what seems to be the problem?'
> Again, Phillip retrieved himself from another narrative and tried to concentrate.

'I'm depressed ... I think I'm depressed,' he said.

'He's very depressed ... aren't you ... Phillip?' Beth asked, placing a hand on his shoulder.

The very touch brought forth a torrent of tears. Phillip covered his face, stifling great gobs of pain.

'Yes,' was all he managed.

At the time I couldn't talk about things much. Even close friends didn't know the full extent of what was happening. People commented later about seeing me walking the kids to school and how I looked on edge, fiercely protective with my arms around them both. The further Aidan sank, the more I tightened my hold on the kids, trying to keep them afloat.

At some point during the worst of those months, I accepted that Aidan might die, that no matter how much therapy he had or how high the dose of antidepressants, nothing could save him from the destructive path he'd started on. And I had to accept that I'd chosen to protect the kids instead of him, because I couldn't do both.

One Sunday afternoon, Aidan met us in a park. The kids hadn't seen him for a few weeks and he was messy. We laid out food and he didn't eat any of it. I remember him watching them play on the equipment and swing from the monkey bars, tears swelling in his eyes. He left after an hour.

He went straight home to his friend's house and locked himself in her spare room and detoxed. Didn't come out again for a couple of days. When he reappeared, he went straight to an AA meeting. And another. And another.

A month later he moved back home. Clean and changed.

Act One: Love

I knew he hadn't done any of it to hurt us, but it still did. And I'd pushed him to the side while the three of us got on with things. Now, I had to learn how to let him back in.

Watching Aidan unravel during that time changed me. It changed us. Before then, we were always equal. He saved me and I saved him. It tipped like a seesaw throughout the years. But for much of 2015, I was squarely stuck on the ground with him dangling up high, his feet never once joining me. And that is an imbalance that took a long time to correct.

I loved Aidan. Fiercely. Completely and resolutely. And slowly we started to edge back together. I remember the day that I realised I wasn't resentful anymore. I'd let it go. I wanted him back in my bed, to be sleeping next to him, with his warm, familiar smell.

Remarkably, that Sunday was the last time he drank. He said he stopped for the kids, so he could be in their lives, so he could have a future. And I can't think about the fact that he recovered from all that – shattering sadness, depression and a period of excessive drinking – only to be diagnosed with terminal cancer three years later. It just doesn't seem fair.

But fairness is a consideration of privilege, pointless really, in the scheme of most people's lives. Talking with the women who cared for him during the worst of that period, we like to marvel at his survival and that he emerged from such darkness to write two of the best plays of his career, reconnect with friends, family and community, be present and loving, and return to his goofy, comedic self.

He was upfront about giving up alcohol, telling friends why and believing that he couldn't drink safely anymore. But it took him several months to stop smoking after he moved back in and it remained his kryptonite until the end.

During the first Covid lockdown in 2020 when Aidan was still upright and managing to climb stairs, clean the house and take short walks, we were trapped together. Like all the families we knew, we couldn't really see anyone else. We relied on each other and mostly it was calm. I'd work a bit, Aidan would sleep a bit, the kids would potter doing schoolwork, and we'd eat dinner and start the whole thing again the next day.

Except Aidan was smoking and trying to hide it.

One night, I woke up to Aidan yelling my name. I ran into the bathroom to find him collapsed on the floor at a strange angle. He'd scraped his back, his leg and his shoulder on the doorframe as he went down. One sniff of the air and I knew it was because he was smoking. He'd managed to get up for a cigarette and tried to blow the smoke out the window but then his leg had given way and he'd crumpled onto the floor.

I slowly helped him up. Helped him back to bed. I snapped that 'if I was dying then having a sneaky cigarette at three in the morning would not be high on my list of priorities'. He was upset, but told me that it helped, smoking helped. It gave him pause, took him momentarily outside himself to a time when he was a different man.

Now I understand more than I did then. Then I was cold and scared and trying to keep him alive. Now I know he was dying and smoking made it easier for him.

Smoking removed him temporarily, gave him something to

look forward to and a way to remember when he was well. But he was bedbound by then and he couldn't smoke cigarettes in bed. When I told him I'd buy him a vape, he laughed.

Hard lockdown meant I couldn't travel any further than five kilometres from our house. I rang my friend and told her to google vapes and find the closest supplier while I drove my streets.

There was one close by. I pulled up out the front. The man wasn't wearing a mask and he had bare feet. I walked in feeling like a teenager, like I was doing something illicit.

I asked the man for the cheapest 'vape machine'. It was clear I had no idea what I was talking about. He told me he had one for 'fifty'. I must have pulled a face because then he said I could have it for 'forty'. I muttered an apology and backed away.

I phoned my friend again and she said there was another shop that might be better.

I drove to the edge of my five-kilometre limit. This time I was greeted with a smile and an explanation of what I needed. It was also only twenty-five dollars. I grabbed flavoured liquids to put into the vape and drove home in a daze.

Towards the final weeks of Aidan's life, our daughter discovered the vape hidden in the folds of the coloured blanket on his bed. I had to explain why it was there, but she knew immediately what it was. Half the kids at school vaped in the toilets. She was amused. Told him it was 'very uncool'.

★

I have often thought about Aidan's *memento mori*: his play *The Architect*, which he started writing before diagnosis but staged after he knew he was dying himself. It was a play written for an older woman called Helen whose house he'd started cleaning after his breakdown. She was a sunflower in a bleak time in Aidan's life. He wasn't writing. He was mopping other people's floors and scrubbing their toilets.

He didn't mind cleaning. A way to earn money, it was meditative and pragmatic and sometimes playful too. He used to clean a friend's place and move little plastic toys into rude positions on the windowsill for her to find. She still laughs whenever she talks about it.

But cleaning Helen's place was something else. It didn't need to be cleaned. She was as fastidious as Aidan was. Mostly they just talked. About books and life. About dying. About losing control. He started writing the play several months after meeting her. The character had the same cancer as her, the same diagnosis. She, too, was smart and funny, independent and mourning her increasing reliance on others.

In an interview for the Melbourne Theatre Company, Aidan said this about the play:

> It's set in Melbourne, now. Housed behind an anonymous-looking front door in a generic-looking suburban street. Our most sacred moments happen almost entirely behind such doors. It's behind these doors that we build our lives. It's also where we destroy them. It's where we are both most trapped and most liberated. Almost everything extraordinary happens behind these ordinary facades.

Act One: Love

In the play, Helen has illegally bought barbital and her son tips it down the sink, not wanting his mother to die. Furious with him, she demands he understands that her death is her choice. It is a heady play, requiring ethical attention, with harrowing drama buried in pitch-perfect comedy.

Aidan too wanted control. But each time he tried to talk to me about it, I struggled. I ducked under the subject, avoiding the possibility that he would want to end his life when he was ready. I couldn't reckon it in my head.

It took the wellbeing woman who worked at the palliative care hospice to challenge me. She questioned why I was having such trouble understanding his wish. Perhaps it was remembering my mum asking me only half jokingly to chop her head off so it would all be over. At the time I knew she was in pain and I didn't want her to be, but I also wanted her to stay.

Death isn't like birth. It doesn't happen over a set timeline. And there's no-one standing by ready to assist if it looks like it's going to take too long. Dying takes time.

Before I watched my mum die, I'd always believed in euthanasia. I was adamant that I would help my loved ones find a peaceful end if I were ever in that position. I remember conversations when Mum and I joked about pushing her wheelchair off a cliff if she made it to a hundred. But it's just not that simple. It's not only a question of legality. Or morality. It's also a question of selfishness.

Even if I'd been able to slip Mum a magic tablet to help her die painlessly in her sleep, would I have done it? I'm no longer so sure.

The process of dying isn't for the patient, it's for those caring for them. I wasn't ready for Mum to die. I needed it to take time. Over those weeks, I needed to process how I was going to feel.

I had to prepare myself for her death and I did it by sitting by her bed day and night, watching her struggle to breathe, refuse to eat and grow angrier and more distant. It was only after watching her suffer that I was fully ready for her to go.

My behaviour was cruel. I know that. I've struggled with that since she died. It surprised me to learn how selfish I was, even though I knew the pain she was in. It shocked me to realise how willing I was to compromise her quality of life just so she could stick around for a bit longer.

We had never really discussed euthanasia until she asked me to chop off her head. We'd had the time, but instead we talked only of the holidays we would have or the nights my children would come and stay with her when she was better. We just never let ourselves go there, preferring to pretend that she would get better. That's the problem with euthanasia. It's only an option if you are prepared to consider your mortality. For my mum, that didn't happen until it was obvious that she wasn't coming home from hospital. And by then it was too late to plan anything as difficult as assisted suicide, especially at a time when it was illegal.

One afternoon my uncle arrived from interstate to farewell my mum, his last remaining sibling. A farmer and a father of a girl who had been very ill as a child, he was pragmatic about saying goodbye. We didn't talk much, but he did comment on how cruel he thought dying was, that 'if she were a cow, they would have shot her by now'. He was right. But that afternoon, sitting next to her in the small room, holding her hand as he said this, I couldn't believe he could be so callous, so unsentimental.

He didn't come to the funeral. He explained that he'd rather say his goodbyes when she was alive than dead, and then he

Act One: Love

hugged me and left. He was practised in the ways of death. He'd shot suffering animals. He'd watched a whole ward of children die, with his daughter the only one to live. He was okay with Mum dying. But I wasn't.

For months before she went into hospital, my mum was so sick she could barely eat. Losing weight rapidly, she was a walking skeleton. I became obsessed with feeding her. I would cook six different dishes, sourcing ingredients like a crazed chef, and then drive the dishes across town, often ignoring the needs of my own young family to try to tempt her with tiny mouthfuls, like a baby bird. It was selfish. She was dying, even then, and we all refused to see it. Instead, I was force-feeding her like I would my four-year-old son when he avoided vegetables for the third day in a row.

The sicker she got, the more I babied her. For a while she was happy with me treating her like a child. And I was happy with that role because if I had something practical to do then I could pretend that I was controlling what happened. I could believe that we were somehow beating the cancer.

The day she went to hospital for the last time was one of the brightest she had over those last months. I sat with her for most of the day, making her eat the hospital food that she clearly didn't want. That day, though, she placated me. She even managed to sit in a chair for two hours and talk. She had a nurse who clearly liked her and kept popping in with little extras to make her comfortable. My mum told stories and the nurse kept returning for more. She wanted my mum's advice on things and my mum clearly loved being asked.

I realised that day that I hadn't asked Mum's advice for months.

Instead, I'd stolen her identity. I'd been so determined she would live, so terrified of considering the possibility she wouldn't, that I'd monologued for six months, and not once had I really asked her anything: what she wanted, if she was scared, if she knew she was dying, if she could tell me what to do.

And that's the thing with dying. For the person doing the dying, they are ahead of the rest of us. They are waiting desperately for the audience to catch up, for us to hopefully find peace before they go, so they can unburden themselves of the conversation. But if we are too scared to see it, then all they can do is make crude jokes about cutting off their head with an axe.

When she was moved into palliative care, she shut me out. She was cross if I turned up with food. She'd stopped eating altogether and it was only to please me that she'd occasionally accept a morsel. She was ready to go. But I still wouldn't let her.

Over the last twenty-four hours of her life, we were all there. My dad, my brother and my brother's partner. Sitting by her bed, not really talking, holding her hand and answering when she'd barely manage to say 'I love you'. That night, we ordered Vietnamese food from down the road and sat in the waiting area eating takeaway, while my mum dozed on and off in her room. I remember thinking how perverse it was that we were fighting over the last spring roll, while she was getting ready to die.

I don't know what I expected death to be. But it wasn't the morphine-induced state that my mother was in. As we crowded around her bed that night, waiting, the nurse kept coming in and commenting on how strong her pulse was. Death didn't seem close. At one point, maybe an hour before she died, she even managed to sit up and pull me down on top of her, whispering in her scratchy, broken voice about how she loved us. And then, over and over, in forced words she asked if it was time.

That night, watching how totally not my mother she had become, I was finally ready. I wanted her to stop breathing. But she kept talking. Trying to tell us to look after each other. And I realised she wasn't quite ready now. We'd somehow swapped positions. Mine was still fuelled by selfishness. I didn't want to watch the agony of it any longer. I just wanted her to go.

And then in thirty seconds, she just stopped breathing. Just like that. No warning. No death rattle. Just silence.

After she died, I was elated. I'd sat in that room for so many weeks and slept on the fold-out chair for so many nights, drunk too many cups of coffee and worried. Suddenly, it was all done. I wasn't consumed anymore. Nothing else was going to happen to her. The worst had come.

We went to the beach that afternoon. Wandered through the streets of my mother's childhood. We ate ice cream and played on the docks. And I felt free.

That feeling lasted a day. The elation was gone by the next morning. When I woke, I was confused. I was ready to go and see her and then I remembered that she wasn't there anymore.

I don't know if we get better at death with practice, but I did come around to Aidan's wish to control his end. I helped him fill in forms and meet with specialists. I had friends witness his sound mind. I learnt how to mix the drugs that would cause his heart to stop. I took control of the key for the locked box. And I asked him each day if he was ready.

And each day he told me, 'Tomorrow. Maybe tomorrow.' But that tomorrow never came. He died without the help.

The pharmacists who came to teach us how to mix the medication and explain how important it was to take the anti-nausea drug first, in case he vomited and ended up in a coma instead of dying, told us that only fifty per cent of people ended up using it. For most, it's a safety net. A support mechanism that means they can relax knowing if things are impossible then they can end it. But only half ever do.

After Aidan died, the pharmacist came to pick up the locked box and the unused medicine. She didn't say it, but I imagine it is a safety precaution so people don't use the drugs themselves. She didn't try to hug me, which I was thankful for, and I handed over the box and closed the door. And it became just another moment in tying up the loose ends of his life.

When we moved house after Aidan died, I found a packet of Nicorette in the cupboard drawer. It was unopened and I was tempted to rip the plastic and pop one out, to chew it, to see if it gave me that buzz, that nicotine rush that Aidan had craved. But they were long past expiry, so instead I tossed them into the bin.

Interval One: A Photograph in Time

There's a photograph of the two of us. We are beaming at the camera. You are hiding your teeth, embarrassed at their state, and I'm flashing mine because I've never learnt how to smile differently. One of us is probably holding the camera up high to avoid the flabby necks that so often appear in selfies.

Your hair is starting to pepper and it's short, too short in patches. Maybe this is around the time I started playing hairdresser at home, trying to save money. My hair is curlier, bigger, fuller than it is now. And it's slightly blonde at the ends from when I still bothered dyeing it. You are wearing that heavy moss-coloured woollen coat we bought second-hand when backpacking in Berlin that is still hanging in my wardrobe. And a bright Kermit-green shirt we no longer have. I'm in something black, as always, but my lips are red with lipstick. Our heads are touching, just enough for there to be no doubt that we are in this together.

What you can't see in the photo is my top stretched tight over my belly, rounded with our first child. You can't see the spare room waiting with a cot and a hand-knitted blanket from my mum, the excited first-time grandmother. You can't see the rented kitchen full of hanging pots and stacked-up plates, home to many dinners. You can't see the outdoor bathroom that we turned into a game. Or the gum tree that loomed large over the backyard.

And you can't see what is yet to come.

This is the photo I would show to a stranger if they wanted to see us as a pair. This snapped image. Of us looking happy. It was the one that led the tribute at your memorial. The one projected before the photos of the four of us. Of our complete little family.

And every time I see it, it undoes me. All that promise of us. All that hope of you and me. All gone.

Act Two: Death

Scene One: Diagnosis

Whenever we were short of money over summer holidays we went camping. Sometimes we'd go with friends and sometimes it would just be the four of us. We pretended we loved the great outdoors, skipping showers and digging a hole to poo, but the truth is that we probably would have preferred booking a holiday house for all of January, driving away with a packed car and no plans to work. Our summers were never that free. Usually, one of us was panicking about money and the other was panicking about writing projects.

January 2018 was no different. We'd made plans to go camping with friends but had left it too late to go into the ballot for one of the prestigious beach sites, so we found something last-minute close to water down along the Great Ocean Road. Just before we left home, Aidan made a doctor's appointment because he'd had a dull pain in his side. I was surprised because he rarely sought medical attention for anything. They ran tests but couldn't find anything wrong and we decided that we'd go camping as planned.

We drove nearly four hours to a new site we hadn't been to before. We set up our tent and our string hammock and arranged our chairs in a large circle. The kids whittled with Swiss Army knives they'd been given for Christmas and we lugged boogie boards up and down the steep hill to float downstream in the little inlet that was brown with the stain of nearby tea-trees. There were snake sightings and late-night marshmallow toastings.

It would be our last family holiday before Aidan was diagnosed.

After you hear news that you know will change everything, you always look back to the moment before. To the ignorant weeks where the worst thing is putting out the rubbish after the bag splits on the way to the bin. You regret that last fight you had and wish you'd done more with the time before cancer smashed its way into your home.

That camping trip wasn't particularly memorable. Just another of the many mini-holidays we'd been on since having the kids. But when we came home, Aidan's back was sore. He started weekly Pilates but it didn't help. So, he went back to the doctor. But this time I made him go to the medical practice where I went. To see a gentle man who prescribed anti-inflammatories before noticing that Aidan had a slightly enlarged lymph node on one side of his neck. The doctor didn't think much of it but suggested a scan. Aidan seemed nonplussed. He wasn't one to over-dramatise anything medical. Unlike me.

On the day of Aidan's scan when he phoned and told me the radiologist had picked up something and they were now doing a

Act Two: Death

biopsy, I knew it was sinister. I even remember where I was when he called me: standing under a gum tree with a red-coloured ribbon around my neck, acting as one of the marshals for the primary school walkathon. After he phoned, I told my friend who I was standing next to that I was worried.

While we waited for biopsy results, we tried to distract each other with life admin. Anything to prevent late-night insomnia and daytime fear. Anything to stop the frantic googling of symptoms. When Aidan's doctor phoned and asked him to come in for an appointment, he refused to let me come. Said he wanted to go alone. We both knew that things were about to change.

I can't remember what I did for the hour or so while I waited for him to return home. I might have been cleaning up the kitchen from the night before or hanging out the washing. I might have been sitting in my favourite chair staring out the window at the grass that needed cutting. I might even have been praying, in my own non-religious way.

But I do remember hearing the key turn in the front door and him crying before he'd even made it down the hallway. I do remember rushing to him as he sobbed that it was metastatic, that the cancer had spread, that it was in his lymph nodes and probably his bones and that it wasn't good. I remember the two of us sinking to the couch, me wrapping myself around him, not knowing what to say or how to be. Him an hour ahead in processing the news and me dragging behind, incapable of believing.

For the next weeks we sat on the diagnosis, not sharing it with anyone. We couldn't agree on how or when to tell the kids. Instead, we pretended that everything was fine. Went to a friend's fiftieth birthday and clutched each other's hands.

I couldn't help but compare it to the other time we sat on a secret for weeks. That time in late 2003 when I was pregnant and we smiled at each other for hours on end, delighting in the thought of having a child. This secret obviously had none of that joy, but it did have the same effect on us as a couple. It drew us close, made us lean into each other, confess our fears, seek out physical intimacy because we were both trying to reassure the other that it would be okay.

Our first cancer appointment was at a public hospital with a urologist. We parked and walked across the road, unsure if the two-hour spot would be long enough. This was the first time Aidan had allowed me in on this medical journey and I was hopeful the specialist would have news we hadn't heard.

We waited. Public hospitals are all about patience and learning to bring a book, charge your phone, have enough money to buy a coffee or top up the parking. That day we had none of our eventual arsenal. We just clutched hands in the waiting room and watched others who looked similarly like ghosts.

Our specialist called us in. We both introduced ourselves. He ignored me. Focused on Aidan. I forgave him immediately because he was the doctor who was about to give us answers. But then he barely looked at Aidan either and instead read from the screen, asked for the origin story of how Aidan had come to be diagnosed. And then he spun on his rotating chair and told us, 'Well, obviously the horse has bolted.'

I gasped. The words were brutal and crude. An analogy used to tell Aidan that he would die and that it was too late to do anything medical. But Aidan wasn't as silenced as I was. In front of us was a man his age, a man at the top of his profession, a man

Act Two: Death

not dissimilar to Aidan. And Aidan wasn't intimidated like I was, which shocked me. I was much more accustomed to medical situations. I was the one who took the kids to the emergency department if they needed it. I was the one who'd had multiple operations and two emergency caesareans and a Pap smear every year or so. There was no part of my body that hadn't been probed or investigated. I wasn't afraid of doctors.

Until now.

The urologist told Aidan he needed to check his prostate by sticking his finger up his rectum. He told Aidan to lay on the bed and then pulled the curtain across so that I could only see the profile of Aidan's face.

I watched as the urologist stretched green surgical gloves onto his hands and then disappeared behind the curtain. Seconds later, he reappeared, telling Aidan to get dressed and that he would need to have his prostate removed immediately.

'How was next week looking?'

My breathing galloped. In. Out. In. Out. Like a metronome a child has played with to speed up time.

We were dismissed. Both of us reeling. Incapable of even comforting each other. There were blood tests and weigh stations and then we were outside. Back in the sunshine. Back on the busy street. Back in the world of the well.

Reaching the car, I gripped Aidan, hugged him, smelt the clove oil on his skin, the mint of stale chewing gum, and I let the air out. He hugged it from me. Squeezing me so close, my lungs emptied. We climbed into the car. Both quiet. Both thinking: how long do we have?

★

It was June when we started to tell people about the cancer. We sat the kids down first on the fading burgundy leather couch in our loungeroom and told them both we had some news.

'Your dad has cancer.'

Our daughter started laughing. It was the third or so time she'd giggled when something shocking had happened. The most recent was when our car had collided with a magpie on the freeway and the headlight had smashed and the magpie had blown off in the wind. That had made her laugh for minutes, until the laughter turned to sobbing.

At first our son didn't comprehend what we were saying. He kept repeating it and asking if we were joking. Aidan played it down. Told them there were plenty of medical options and he was feeling great, but that he'd have to have chemotherapy soon.

They both seemed stuck on the idea that Aidan's hair would fall out. He still had that quiff of thick hair that I'd been so taken with the first time I saw him, only now it was more white than black. He promised he'd try the ice cap that a friend had used and that maybe his hair would be fine.

The conversation stalled. It was clear the kids couldn't process any more of it, so we walked to the gelato place for double scoops.

It makes no sense now that we chose that moment to take a family stroll for a Sunday afternoon ice cream, but that was all part of us struggling to know how to cope. We wanted to hit the pause button and slow everything down and pretend just for a minute that things were *normal*.

★

Act Two: Death

But we couldn't. In the words of the specialist, the horse had bolted. When a well-connected friend told us she knew a urologist, someone her brother had gone through school with, we decided we wanted a second opinion. She rang him. He agreed to see us after consulting hours that week.

Hopeful for more optimistic news, we drove to Hawthorn. I whined about the other urologist and this specialist admitted he knew the man had a reputation for an unorthodox bedside manner. But despite being gentler with the news, the verdict was the same. He said there was no point removing the prostate because the horse really had bolted. The cancer couldn't be treated. Slowing it was the only possible course. Aidan was referred to an oncologist who would be our doctor for the next two years.

Our road through the medical system was not without endless frustrations, but it was always helped by the fact we were educated and white, and that we knew people who knew people. I cannot imagine being embroiled in the system without having confidence or speaking English, because it is a system that benefits those who push and agitate. I don't mean yelling 'It's my turn!' when in a waiting room. I mean not being afraid to phone a doctor or a hospital for answers, for truth, for medicine. Being an advocate for your own body takes such effort when you are terminally ill and if there is not a person in your corner who can do it for you, then you are left behind.

But advocating for your partner takes its toll too. It changes things between you. Things you don't see at the time. Until Aidan was diagnosed, we were joined in our plans for the future. We believed we would watch our children grow, celebrate their independence when they became adults, enjoy our time as a couple again, travel, work, argue, live. Suddenly I was the only one with a future. We were now on different clocks.

Aidan and I had always looked after each other. We may have had different ways of demonstrating 'I love you', but we understood both of our languages. He would bring me hot water bottles and cups of coffee in bed and I'd do his tax each year. He would help fix the structural issues in my work and I would check his grammar. I would cook and he would clean. He would joke and I would laugh. We worked together.

But a terminal cancer diagnosis changed all that.

It's not just that you know the person will die sooner than you'd always imagined, it's that it becomes very hard to think about anything else because it is now framed through a different lens, one that weighs heavily. You can't just go on a holiday; you have to make memories. You can't just start writing a new play because you probably won't be here to finish it. You can't think about your children turning eighteen because you will be long gone.

Grief starts before the person you love dies. It starts the moment they are told the cancer will kill them.

Scene Two: Shame

One of the first things people ask when someone has been diagnosed with cancer is: 'What sort?' Like that matters. Like that determines how much we should care.

The problem with that question is that for the cancer patient, answering it can trigger many emotions, including shame.

Aidan was educated in the language of shame from his years spent in the Catholic Church, but I was raised free of religion and was a young adult before I really understood the concept.

The night that taught me about shame began as just another Friday. I was eighteen, on a night out with my part-time flatmate, a friend who was grieving the recent death of her dad. She lived in the inner city and I stayed over on weekends. We never cooked and rarely ate meals, but each payday she'd shop for fancy snacks at an expensive department store. Sometimes I'd bring her the rescued loaves of Boston buns from the bakery I worked in and we'd run our hands along the tops, gathering fake icing and hard-crusted coconut to lick off our fingers.

Back then, I wore a pastel pink suit bought for a family wedding and my hair was long and straight, tinted blonde in the sun. Back then, I smiled on command and danced my Friday nights away listening to some ageing piano-man sing songs from the past. Back then, my dreams of who I was didn't align with the suburban girl who let her mum do her washing.

My friend's cheeks flushed red when she was nervous or excited.

Her hair was short and bouncy.

She was lean and muscled and unlike anyone I'd met before.

Once, when we were out, she flagged down a car of young guys and fleeced them for cash.

At the time, I'd convinced myself I was there for her, holding her hand as she struggled with grief. But looking back, I'm not sure she needed anyone.

Now I know I was there for me. For adventure. For adrenaline. Staying with her was like standing on the edge of a building, wondering if you were about to be pushed.

That Friday, we were at the club we always went to. The older man she was sleeping with turned up, like he usually did. And there was another man too. I'm not sure now if they were real friends or if they just knew each other from work, but suddenly there were two of them. A multiplication of older men.

We were comfortably drunk.

We left that club and went to another.

The men seemed to know people. We didn't queue to get in. Drinks kept appearing in our hands. The men had connections.

At some point, my friend was lost to me.

Act Two: Death

I danced a little with the other man. And on the mezzanine level, we kissed. I remember there were couches – plush, velvet maybe, stained with spilt drinks that had crusted in patches. I don't remember talking, but maybe we did.

I was still learning about sex. I'd messed around a bit with a few high-school boyfriends. Made it to some base or another. I could flirt, but I couldn't follow through. I was mouthy when it came to an argument, silent when it came to my body.

Someone I'd known when I was little had tried to pick me up at one of these clubs. He'd bought me a giant book of Snoopy cartoons and wrapped it for my sixth birthday. I couldn't find the words when he hit on me, obviously forgetting our distant connection. He hadn't seen me since I was a child, and I didn't remind him of Snoopy. I just gaped, like a fish out of water, shocked and flailing. And then I ducked away and hid in the toilets. Anything to avoid confronting him.

It was those nights in that club that shook me into adulthood, ripped me from the sleepy suburb I'd grown up in where I'd plastered posters of tennis players I'd loved on my walls, and plunged me into high alert.

With little experience of touching bodies that weren't the skinny and undeveloped boys of my high school, I let this man glide his hands over me while he pushed me back on that velvet crusted couch.

When my friend reappeared, she was smiling, pleased I'd found someone. She said we were going back to her place. All four of us. After arriving at the flat, the couples split. We could hear my friend having sex through the thin curtain that separated us.

I worried the man I was with expected the same. I was right.

I know there was no condom. No question. No stopping.

I know that in the morning he was gone. I was hungover. Scared. Unsure of what had happened.

I know that I left before my friend awoke.

I know it was the Queen's Birthday long weekend and the streets were quiet. I know I had to walk to reach my car where I'd left it parked the night before.

I know I didn't consent, but I was confused about what that meant.

The drive home to my parents took nearly an hour. A freeway and then miles of bends and sweeping hills. So much time to think.

I parked my little run-down Fiat where I always parked. On the flat of the hill, just above the fading campervan that we'd used for fraught family holidays. Mum met me on the brick verandah wearing her green terry-towelling dressing-gown, pleased to see me home.

I didn't know how to tell her I'd had sex with an older man I'd just met. A man I'd let touch my breasts. A man I'd taken home to my friend's flat.

I couldn't even admit it to myself.

I was terrified of diseases and pregnancy. This was the tail end of the eighties when the grim reaper loomed on our television screens and AIDS was a fierce shadow.

I showered, washing him off me.

I drank coffee and refused food.

I started shutting down.

Convinced I had every sexually transmitted disease going, I saw a doctor, stuck out my arm for blood tests, lay on the bed for swabs and didn't watch as they labelled the vials for pathology.

Act Two: Death

I tried to forget the man with the nice suit and the white-toothed smile. The man with the metal clip securing his bundle of cash. The man whose name was 'Simon' or 'Stuart' or something like that. The man who didn't listen when I said 'No'.

No.

No, no, no.

The doctor rang. The tests were all negative. I wasn't pregnant. I wasn't sick. Not physically anyway.

I didn't tell my friend, but we were not the same after that. I stopped sleeping over. I stopped sleeping. I made up reasons for staying home on the weekends. I took up smoking. I buried my shame.

As I write this now, I know it was rape. Perhaps, I knew it then too, but in my eighteen-year-old head, it didn't have a name. I blamed myself. I led him on. Took him home. Let him kiss me. And more. I couldn't reconcile it with the rapes I'd heard discussed. The violent and the frightening. Mine was in the safety of my friend's flat. In my eighteen-year-old-head, mine wasn't worthy of discussion.

In his writings about the psychology of shame, German philosopher Friedrich Nietzsche talks not only about the shame that a sufferer experiences, but also about the shame that someone who witnesses the sufferer's shame feels. This secondary shame can lead to pity. I didn't tell my mum about my rape because I was embarrassed that it had happened and I didn't want her to see me differently, to judge me, to pity me. I didn't want her to try to make it okay.

When Aidan was first diagnosed, a couple of friends were also being treated for cancer. I remember going to the pub with one of them and how we tried to keep it light because we were all acutely aware that Aidan was going to die but they were not.

As friends, we do not want to see the people we love suffering, struggling or even being vulnerable to the extent that it challenges our own sense of mortality. I think for Aidan this was often alienating, this aloneness in the experience he was having.

Shame is a powerful silencer. To preserve a sense of our perfect image, shame can cause us to lie and to create elaborate fictional narratives in which to deal with the rawness of our emotions and with the judgements of others.

In 1989, American Professor Kenneth J Doka coined the term 'disenfranchised grief' to explain the emotion experienced by mourners when there is no social recognition to their right to grieve openly. Doka categorised disenfranchised grief into five types. The first is when the relationship isn't acknowledged, in the case of an ex-partner or ex-spouse, or possibly an illicit relationship like an affair. The second is when the loss itself isn't recognised, in the case of mourning the death of a relationship. The third occurs when the griever isn't acknowledged because of the grieving person's age or perceived inability to understand their loss. The fourth is for reasons of societal or cultural stigma like in the case of death through suicide or addiction. And the last is when the person's grief process doesn't fit with

Act Two: Death

the expectations of society, perhaps because of their cultural response to grief.

I heard Doka interviewed during the height of the Covid pandemic when he was discussing the shame some people felt when their relatives died of Covid, as if mourning was not complicated enough without adding another layer to their loss. He gave the example of communities in the US where people did not take the risk of Covid seriously, so that sometimes after a death due to Covid, the community would shift the blame from the virus onto the person who had died. For some mourners, the shame was so great that instead of organising a funeral, they buried their family members quickly, hoping to avoid questions about how they died. He compared it to the blame associated with dying of HIV back in the nineties. Then we had 'innocent victims', like haemophiliacs who'd received a contaminated blood transfusion, as opposed to 'guilty ones' who had contracted AIDS through unprotected sex.

It is confronting to face our own mortality, so we invent protection. We can mourn tragic accidents because the risk of it happening to us is low. But we struggle with cancer deaths in people our age because we fear it could be us next. So, we find a way to feel safe. We make it the dying person's fault. We aren't necessarily aware of this, but I imagine the person who has been diagnosed is.

And perhaps that is where the shame comes in.

When my mum was diagnosed with lung cancer, she was full of rage. She'd never smoked. She didn't drink. She was healthy and fit and felt it should be happening to someone else. Her response impacted on me too, and whenever I mentioned her diagnosis to other people, I always prefaced it with the fact that her lung cancer was the type to strike those who had never smoked. Why did it matter? Lung cancer would kill her, so why did I feel I needed to present her as blameless? Was her death any more harrowing than if she'd smoked?

Lung cancer patients feel this shame acutely because there is a perception that it is their fault. My mum felt that even as a non-smoker. I cannot imagine how a smoker must feel.

But the shame was not just created by a public perception of her illness, but also of her own body. She couldn't breathe properly. Her lungs hurt. She couldn't walk far. She wasn't hungry. The chemotherapy made her take to bed for weeks on end. She was ashamed because her body was failing her.

And I was ashamed because I struggled when I had to lift her to the toilet, when I had to help her dress, when I had to hold a vomit bag so she could be sick. I was ashamed of my reaction to her failing body. She must have felt my shame. And yet for two people who had shared such intimate lives for so long and had been honest about such painful things, this was off limits to us.

I still feel shame that I couldn't tackle this with her at the time.

Hearing Professor Doka discuss shame made me think about Aidan and how he'd approached his diagnosis. The shame he felt was to do with being a man. We are told that prostate cancer is an illness developed by men towards the end of their lives, not by a man at the height of his power who prides himself on being physical and in his body. By framing it as an older man's disease, young men feel safe because they believe it won't happen to them.

But it does. All the time.

Act Two: Death

Aidan and I didn't talk about prostate cancer very much. It was a wedge between us. The injections to stop testosterone killed his sexual desire. His cancer became something that kept us apart intimately. We tried to have conversations about us as a couple, but they were loaded and painful. He felt he was failing me because we weren't having sex. But for me it wasn't his cancer that was preventing us, it was how he felt about himself. His back hurt, he was on serious medication, he struggled to look at himself in the mirror. And his shame came from knowing that his body had failed him and fearing that he was somehow broken or faulty.

I think he felt that he'd become someone I cared about medically, rather than someone I was intimate with physically. And it was such a huge gap to repair that we couldn't. Not while we both grieved what we knew was coming.

A man we knew only from holidaying at the same place each year joked when I explained Aidan's diagnosis. He made some crass comment about his 'pecker not working', and I had to walk away before I punched him. I've often thought about that moment since, wishing I'd swung a sharp left hook and cracked his nose, or at least confronted him verbally and unpacked what he was feeling about his own mortality, sexuality and manhood. But I didn't. I crept away, ashamed. Ashamed for Aidan and for me.

To that man, and many others, prostate cancer is the worse diagnosis imaginable, even though most people live for many years managing it. It is not impossible to be sexually active after a prostate diagnosis but when the diagnosis is already metastatic it adds complicated psychological layers to intimacy. Pain can interfere with the desire to be touched and it can be hard to hold on to the idea of yourself as someone sexual when you no longer recognise your own body.

After Aidan started having the injections and his skin became hairless and his face lost its daily bristle, he struggled with the physical changes. He hated becoming soft. Skin, chest, arms – everything changed. It was difficult. For us, for him, for me. Made worse by the fact that it was just something we couldn't quite expose to each other.

It made me consider a friend who'd had a double mastectomy after her breast cancer diagnosis and how she'd grappled with her changed body. She talked about it, admitted how confronting it was to see her chest. Perhaps women are more equipped to confront the changes in their bodies caused by cancer because they are so often changed by periods, pregnancy, breastfeeding, age.

Many of us will be diagnosed with a form of cancer at some point in our lives. And it will alter us physically. The chemotherapy will cause our hair to fall out. It might affect our voice, the nerves in our fingers, our limbs, our organs. And yet we continue to 'other' those with cancer because it makes us feel safe.

As Aidan grew sicker and his body grew weaker, he surrendered to it and I to him. I rubbed cream into his feet and stroked his hair. I helped him to the toilet when he could still stand, and then when he couldn't, I pulled adult-sized nappies up his thinning legs, trying not to knock a joint or touch a pain spot so he wouldn't wince or cry out.

Sometimes it was this that made me sob as I left his room.

Act Two: Death

Seeing his body so changed. Even now, I try to avoid thinking of that time unless I want to cry.

When I have a quiet moment I find myself desperate to remember parts of him. From before. His forearms, browned with the sun and freckled. The man up a ladder, changing light bulbs. The man under a car, fixing something. The man with a record playing, volume up high, mopping the floors until they gleamed, knowing nobody else would do it. The man I shared my bed with for all those years, whose arms would wrap tight around me.

The man I loved.

Scene Three:
A Tabby

Apparently, there are more pets than people living in Australia and ninety per cent of Australian households have had a pet at some time. As a child, I was not represented by these statistics. I was in the ten per cent who did not have a registered pet.

    I'd grown up in the outer-eastern suburbs of Melbourne where the Yarra River wound its mighty way through the bush. The suburb of Wonga Park was built on orchards and bushland, and we had a small quarter-acre block carved from something larger, living in a house that Mum had designed based on others she'd seen by local architect Alistair Knox. She had no formal qualifications and had left school at fourteen, but she knew what she liked and was skilled at drawing scaled sketches from her years of pattern making for clothes. Ahead of its time, the house was built from recyclable materials: old Hawthorn Black bricks rescued from a city demolition, wooden sleepers reclaimed from disused railway lines and cold blue-grey slate that lined the floors. It wasn't just about re-using the old, it was also about saving money. The house was surrounded by windows that looked out onto the overgrown garden and I woke most mornings to birdsong and the whisper of the trees.

My parents planted their land out with native trees, nursing a fledgling lemon-scented gum through the cold winters with plastic bags covering its leaves to protect it from the frost. Over the years, they converted their empty block from a decimated colonial orchard back to its indigenous roots. With the native trees and shrubs came echidnas, blue-tongue lizards, tawny frogmouths and snakes. Brown and black, the snakes would lie on the warm bluestones in the winter sun. We knew to avoid them, but we were never scared of them. Just aware.

As kids, we marched in anti-nuclear rallies, dressed in clothes Mum sewed for us and were not allowed to have domestic pets. I could ride horses on the weekends, but they were owned by the pony club and never by me. Instead, we pretended the echidna that curled in our front yard and the resident blue-tongue lizard that hid under the bluestones were ours.

By the time I moved out of home, I wasn't a fan of cats or dogs, ranting smugly about it to anyone who would listen. When my friend brought her grey tabby Mika to live with us in our flat, I ignored it. Mika tried to bond with me, rubbing against my legs as if she was daring me to enjoy it. But I held fast to my upbringing, complaining about the native birds deposited on our back step by the cat. Luckily my friend was more tolerant of me than I was of her cat and mostly found me amusing.

My children, however, did not. While their friends lived in

houses with never-ending pet adoptions, I tried to instil a love of the nature found in our backyard. Snail race, anyone?

Aidan had grown up with all sorts of animals, including a pet cow he used to joke was slaughtered for dinner. In 2016, he convinced me to adopt a huge tank full of exotic fish that had been a prop in one of his plays. Our daughter loved testing the pH levels of the water and cleaning the tank, which took most of a day every month, but still the fish slowly died. It turned out that the large, bottom-feeding catfish wasn't just snacking on the specialist dried food, it was also swallowing most of its cellmates.

Renting meant I could always blame the landlord for our lack of pets. And I managed to win with that argument for some years. Then in April 2020, everything changed. At that time, we'd survived a month into the first lockdown and Aidan's doctors had decided that he wasn't responding well enough to the radical trial he was on, so it was time to take him off.

With the trial, Aidan had discovered hope during his diagnosis. He clung to it. We sat in meetings with department heads of clinical trials, hearing about how cancer had shrunk in some of the patients after they'd finished a course of lutetium and Aidan would come home confident that if he could just be approved for the clinical trial, he too would see results.

He was approved for the trial. The trial our son called 'The Hulk' because it made Aidan radioactive for a few days after each dose. Lutetium is the highest-melting rare-earth metal. Atomic number 71, it is silvery-white in colour. It is used in men with metastatic prostate cancer when all other forms of treatment have failed. It doesn't cure cancer, but it may shrink tumours and slow their growth. Prostate-specific membrane antigen (PSMA) is a

Act Two: Death

protein found on the surface of a cell. Patients with prostate cancer have more PSMA than normal. The therapy uses a molecule that attaches to the PSMA receptors on the cancer cells and tries to destroy the prostate cancer cells in a targeted way. It means that rather than exposing your whole body to radiation, the PSMA molecule sends the lutetium directly to the cancer sites. But PSMA is also found in salivary glands, kidneys and the small intestine, so the molecule can send radiation to these areas too.

Aidan had burning in his mouth and his urine was radioactive for up to thirty days after each dose. I was told not to sleep next to him for a few nights and that he should use his own bathroom. We didn't have another bathroom. Each time he had a dose of lutetium, he would stay at a friend's empty flat for a few nights so that we weren't all dosed in his radioactivity. It also gave us both a break.

Lutetium had little effect on Aidan's cancer. It barely slowed the tumours or reduced their growth. When he finished the trial, he was spat out the other end of a system that has little time for emotional follow-ups. Plus, Covid had hit and the hospital didn't see patients face to face anymore. It was all done on telehealth.

The trial was a last-ditch attempt at stalling the cancer that by now had spread through much of his spine and into his sacrum. It was painful for Aidan to walk and increasingly harder for him to find a comfortable way to sleep. Aidan propped himself up with pillows so that he could sit at the dinner table but he often wasn't very hungry.

We both knew what this meant. If the trial had failed, there were no other options. His body couldn't cope with more chemotherapy, and radiotherapy would only be used if the pain spots hadn't already been zapped multiple times, which they had. The cancer couldn't be slowed. He was in the last stage of his life.

Aidan was so shattered by the medical news that I offered to be the one to break it to the kids. I'd had this uncomfortable, prickly feeling in my skin for days because I knew the kids weren't aware of how sick Aidan was. Even though he was having trouble walking and he was losing weight and sleeping much of the day, they were clinging to the idea that he would improve.

Aidan and I had always tried to balance that line between honesty with the kids and not overloading them with too much adult information. I knew it was time to tell them the truth, but the truth meant hurting them and changing the way they interacted with their dad. It's hard being 'normal' with someone who's dying. I struggled to build the same relationship with Aidan after he was diagnosed. Even unconsciously, I became the carer and the keeper of secrets while he was freer to feel. I chose the role of someone trying to stop my family from crumbling. I knew that the kids would shift their interactions with him without even realising they were doing it, and I knew what that would do to Aidan.

I told them separately, maybe because I was too scared to tell them together. Or maybe because I knew I wouldn't be able to comfort them both at the same time. Or perhaps because I knew that they'd want different answers because they were three-and-a-half years apart.

I have no memory of who I told first, but I will never forget their reactions.

There had always been bed-hopping in our house – one of us booted out of our big bed in the middle of the night by a sick child, a child with a nightmare or a child just wanting a cuddle.

Act Two: Death

With the anxiety of lockdown, online schooling and Aidan's illness, the bed hopping was frequent. The night I told our son, he'd been sharing the big bed with me for a few nights and Aidan had taken our son's room. It was late and our son couldn't sleep.

That night, we started whispering about how sick his dad was. I couldn't really see my son's face, could just make out the shape of his twelve-year-old body. Knowing that he's not one to enjoy being pinned down and made to discuss serious issues, I skirted around the topic for a while. And then, using the shield of the dark room and the fact that we couldn't look at each other clearly, I told him that his dad was going to die.

He has never been a crier. He usually keeps his emotions tightly bundled. But that night he sobbed. He shook and clung to me, his arms sticky and smooth in the way that young kids are. We just lay in the dark and cried. Each time I thought he'd stopped, he would gasp for air and start up all over again.

The next day it was like it never happened. He reverted to his generally buoyant self and I couldn't work out how to bring it up again. It just festered under the surface like mould. He knew. I knew. Aidan knew. But we couldn't quite reach each other to talk about it more.

When I told our daughter, she was equally distressed but, between the tears, she wanted facts. She wanted to know how long and what had changed in his prognosis. I found myself struggling to answer because nobody knew the answers. She wanted to know if he'd make it to Christmas and I had to tell her it was probably unlikely.

After I told her, we walked for hours in the dark around the quiet streets of Brunswick. It was one of those conversations I've returned to many times. She was so adult in her dissection of her feelings. So capable at identifying what and how this news had changed her. But she was also in shock. She'd always thought her dad would be around until she reached eighteen and now she had to shift her whole thinking.

She took to her bed with a pile of classics and read, not bothering to answer text messages or communicate with the world. She stopped attending online school and started reading *Anna Karenina*.

While she read, our son disappeared into the garage to play drums for hours each day until a neighbour banged on the door and told him to stop.

And I got busy. I ran up and down the stairs with meals and snacks so many times that eventually my knees swelled and ached.

Because busyness stopped me from feeling.

Sensing how off my game I was and prompted by a friend fostering a litter of kittens, the kids presented me with a PowerPoint presentation and essay on why we needed a pet. Full of colourful photos, clever graphics and convincing arguments, it was perhaps the only schoolwork they did that month, which helped increase its impact. I reluctantly agreed. And without feeling like there was any other way of healing my family or of bringing them together in their grief, I added a cat.

We adopted a tabby kitten from the Lost Dogs Home. She'd been fostered by a friend who'd patiently delivered her to us for short visits, as if she knew I had to test out the territory before committing. The day we collected her from the shelter in a

Act Two: Death

borrowed carrier, both kids came with me. They waited outside in the rain because Covid restrictions meant only one person could go in. They fought over who would carry the cargo to the car. My son won and sat in the back, talking to the kitten through the mesh grill. She meowed all the way home – little gulps of air and worry – and I wondered what I'd got us into.

Online schooling stalled as both kids spent their days fighting over the kitten. They watched in delight as she raced around the room, tearing it up with all the fearlessness and foolishness of a young child. Aidan let her scratch his arms and play rough while I tried to train her. We battled over names and finally agreed on Beanie.

Before, we were like four different spinning wheels, each with our own rhythm and speed, not intersecting except when we crashed hard into each other and knocked the other off their axis. But Beanie became a manic, kitten-style glue that kept us all from moving too far apart. At night, we'd spread along the couch and take it in turns to toss toys in the air and watch her chase them. I still hadn't quite worked out how I felt about having a cat in the house. But to Aidan and the kids she was a lifeline.

About two months after Beanie came to live with us, she skidded through the gap between the stairs and dropped six feet onto another staircase. She landed awkwardly and couldn't bear weight on her front right leg, hobbling around the room.

Until then I'd tolerated Beanie's presence in the house, frustrated by her clawing at my furniture and trying to eat the indoor plants. But that day, that moment when I thought she was injured, I did what I do best. I tried to fix it. I rang every vet in the area until I found one who would see her instantly. I drove her there with our son playing distraction in the back seat.

As we pulled up outside the vet, I knew that I'd pay whatever it took for her to be okay. I'd crossed over from that neurotic adult who never touched cats or patted dogs to someone who loved their household pet like a third child.

The vet was kind and understanding. He sold me anti-inflammatory drops and told me to watch her for a day or two before doing an X-ray. He thought she'd be fine and she was. But I wasn't. I came home and spent the day taping the holes between the stairs with gaffer tape and hand-cut cardboard lengths so she could never fall again. I fed her poached chicken and let her sleep on my bed. She was cold and uninterested in us much of the time, like cats seem to be. But occasionally, and only when it suited her, she'd curl up on a lap, or hide under a doona, or stare at us with those green unblinking eyes.

Our daughter told me that having Beanie meant she could take the cat to visit Aidan in his makeshift hospital room and pretend the cat was the reason she was paying him a visit, not the fact that he couldn't get up anymore. Beanie provided everyone with an excuse. To cuddle. To talk. To just be.

The day before Aidan died, Beanie left her usual sleeping place on the end of his bed by the window, where the afternoon winter sun shone through the glass. That day, she curled up on the floor and stayed there, sleeping near the motor that powered the self-inflating air mattress the palliative care nurse had fitted to stop Aidan needing to be rolled so often.

When the nurse arrived to show me how to use the morphine driver, I pointed out Beanie's new place of rest. The nurse smiled

Act Two: Death

and told me that cats often knew when the time was close. Perhaps Beanie had worked out something we hadn't.

Beanie was still on the floor when Aidan died the next day. But for the days after, while I waited for hospital equipment to be collected and carpets to be steamed clean, she avoided that room, as if sensing his absence and understanding her place was to now help us heal.

Beanie is our link to before. Before Aidan died. Before he was bedbound. Before he was a shell of medicine and sadness.

And in a claws-out, meowing sort of way, she has softened our grief and filled some of Aidan's absence to become the fourth member of our little family.

Scene Four: Lasts

Nobody really knows when someone is going to die. Even oncologists can only estimate based on other patients and research. So much of it depends on the individual. Which may explain why at first I missed the signs.

Three months before Aidan died in September 2020, I was out with the kids and he rang to tell me that he'd scrubbed the rug and managed to haul it out to the balcony, but that it was too heavy to lift over the railing. In a smaller voice, he said he'd have to wait for me to help him and then asked when I was coming home.

He'd never asked me to help with something physical, something he could have done alone once. It was a turning point for us. A reminder that it wasn't just Covid lockdowns causing changes, but that things inside our house were different too.

Because Aidan and I were so preoccupied with his cancer, neither of us could enforce parenting rules. Television was watched nightly, breakfast was eaten late and nobody seemed to go to bed before eleven. We considered showering a weekly event. Online schooling meant the kids were strapped to computer screens, wandering upstairs for snacks when they were on a break. I spent much of my time preparing meals, cleaning the kitchen then preparing more.

Friends cooked so that I didn't have to. They delivered still-warm gnocchi and banana bread threaded with chocolate, a lump of French cheese and pizza dough. These deliveries were small interruptions in miserable days. They meant that for the time it took us to unpack, inspect and sample, we'd forget why they were being delivered in the first place. With each arrival of food, we could pretend we were leaving the house, imagining the warmth of other people's kitchens and travelling to new lands.

I think their arrival sometimes embarrassed Aidan. They acted as a reminder of his neediness, his illness. But for the three of us, they were a much-wanted distraction and sometimes the only outside contact we had.

Even with the financial support of generous friends, we couldn't afford for both of us not to work, and I had book contracts to fulfil and a future to consider. Some days I hid downstairs in the garage with my laptop on the soft green couch that Aidan had managed to deliver in the back of our old Subaru just months before.

The writing took me away from the rest of the house. It meant I could dive into a world where lockdowns didn't exist, where my characters could test out relationships and fight with parents who were not sick. I remember writing a camping scene where three characters shared a tent, and being struck by how foreign that idea was because we were still masked up and social distancing.

I finished two books during that period. The historical time-slip *Elsewhere Girls*, which I co-wrote with a friend who would meet me in the park to share a thermos of negroni and talk through plot. And *The Edge of Thirteen*, the third in a series, which meant the characters and world were already so familiar it felt more like catching up with old friends than inventing new ones.

But writing was hard during those months. I had to carve out time to care about creating something that would only come to life after Aidan had died. He had always been a valued contributor, and now I was on my own.

While Aidan was still well enough to be left, I took advantage of my allocated exercise time like most of us did in locked-down Melbourne and met different friends each day to wind our way through familiar streets, sipping coffee. I clung to those small outings, those moments where I could see the sky, feel the breeze, talk openly and sometimes cry. I forged deeper friendships on those walks, enjoying the freedom of side-by-side conversations that we know is the trick to encouraging teenagers to talk. The bleakness of what was happening at home, and the strangeness of our pandemic lives, made us seek out topics we usually wouldn't.

Even as we lived it, that time was a blur. Days bled into each other, marked only by Aidan's slowing down. His winter of lasts: the last time he drove, the last time he made his own coffee, the last time he walked.

Act Two: Death

The last time we went out together without the children.

We'd been sent a voucher for groceries from the Victorian Actors' Benevolent Trust, an organisation that helps those in the industry when things are tough. It was a Friday afternoon and I was writing an epic shopping list to buy with the voucher. The kids were adding random things like noodles and ice cream, jelly snakes and apple juice. I wrote down all of it. In the space of weeks, I'd gone from being a granola mum to an 'eat whatever you like' mum.

As I packed the car with shopping bags, Aidan came out of the house. He wanted to come too. 'A sort of date,' he said. Understanding his ache for normalcy, I smiled and tossed the bags in the back, making room for him in the passenger seat. He usually hated it when I drove, but he'd accepted that his time behind the wheel had ended.

We didn't go to the usual supermarket at the end of the street. A date deserved more effort and I drove the quiet streets to the second-closest.

Aidan was wearing a white mask with bright red apples on it that a friend had made him. It fit him perfectly, the loops of elastic sitting neat around his ears. His hair was fluffy and upright, and he had so many layers on he seemed to move stiffly as we walked up and down the aisle.

There was a recklessness to our shopping, as we tossed in items that we didn't need, didn't want and would never buy if we weren't in limbo. At first, we joked, holding hands and egging each other on, filling the troller higher and higher until I had to take over pushing it because the wheels had their own plan and Aidan wasn't strong enough to stop it from careering wildly.

Before we'd had the kids, we often ended our nights out buying snacks to eat on the couch. Now we were back in a grimly lit supermarket, pretending we were still those people.

But then Aidan started limping through the dairy section and I suggested he wait in the car while I finished up. He growled at me, angry and impatient. I bit back and pushed the trolley past him, speeding up because I knew he couldn't.

The date was over.

I used the voucher, bagged the shopping and struggled to carry everything to the car by myself.

He was crying before I could even start the ignition. Sobbing into his hands, words bubbled out, messy and unclear: 'Contribute ... Helpful ... Useless ...' I understood. He was unmoored. He had no role left. Except patient. And that had never suited him. He'd always been able. And now he couldn't even shop.

That was our last date. Our last outing, except for the hospital visits, which only cemented my role as carer and his as someone who needed one.

The last time we ever left the house together was for the final dose of radiotherapy. The cancer had spread down his spine and had stopped him from being able to walk. At that stage, if we wanted to eat dinner with him, we'd have to carry it all downstairs to his bedroom. A month earlier, he was still cleaning the house, climbing the stairs, vacuuming twice a day as he'd always done. The disability had seemed to happen almost overnight.

We'd developed a system for the radiotherapy visits. I'd park the car, head upstairs to where the bank of hospital wheelchairs lived and take one back to the car park where I'd help him manoeuvre his legs and lift himself in. Covid protocols meant nothing was quick. I had to scan QR codes, have my temperature checked and change my homemade mask for a disposable hospital one. Then we had to do it all again when we came back upstairs with the wheelchair.

On our last visit, as I wheeled Aidan towards the nurse on the radiotherapy floor, she smiled and said hello. We were all masked so her greeting was muffled, but it was something – a new face, an interaction with a stranger, a kindness. She wheeled Aidan away because I wasn't allowed any further and I sat in one of the waiting areas, watching the television screen, trying not to feel. I'd become an expert in shutting down. I could manage a whole day of caring and cleaning and cooking without feeling anything. But when I ran into people I knew, they'd tilt their head to the side and ask in soft tones how I was going. And I'd tell them it was fine. We were fine. *I* was fine.

Visiting the hospital made it harder to pretend because illness was everywhere. It was a cancer hospital. Bald heads, IV drips, wheelchairs, people with that expression that you learn to recognise. I didn't like coming here. It was difficult to stop myself from feeling when I walked through these doors.

But at least here, we were just another cancer case, another patient, another carer, another person in the system. I was relieved when the administration staff were rude, or when we were sent to the wrong floor, or when we were kept waiting for hours. That meant we were the same as everyone else.

★

That last time in the hospital while I was sitting waiting for him with the television explaining the latest Covid numbers, I heard a child scream as they headed into radiotherapy and the sound was sobering. Sick adults were one thing, but sick children were another.

Then the nurse wheeled Aidan out and I stood to take my place behind the handles of the wheelchair. As we swapped roles, the nurse smiled at me and said, 'How lovely that you've brought your father in for treatment.'

I blinked, processing her words, realising after a second that she thought I was Aidan's daughter, even though I was in my scruffy uniform of those lockdown months, probably braless, with unbrushed, unwashed, uncut hair and no make-up.

I wheeled him away quickly and he looked up and over the back of the wheelchair at me, his grey hair soft and floppy, his eyes amused.

'Daughter,' he said, with a grin.

And we laughed all the way to the lift because we hadn't laughed in ages.

Scene Five: Kissing

According to psychologist John Bohannon and his research team from Butler University in the US, most of us can remember up to ninety per cent of the details of a first romantic kiss. This is irrespective of age or where and when the kiss occurred.

I cannot clearly remember my first kiss with Aidan. Or the details of the many kisses that came after. Just that they were part of us, part of our everyday. He was a little taller than me and he didn't love kissing like I did. Perhaps because he hated his teeth and never revealed them in a smile.

In her book *The Science of Kissing: What Our Lips Are Telling Us*, science journalist Sheril Kirshenbaum traces the first historical literary reference of romantic kissing to India's Vedic Sanskrit texts of 1500 BCE. Other researchers believe it dates back even further, citing mentions on clay tablets from Mesopotamia. Kirshenbaum also references a study conducted by British zoologist Desmond Morris in which he showed photographs of women wearing various shades of lipstick to male volunteers and asked them to rate the women's attractiveness. The women wearing the brightest and reddest lipstick were voted the most attractive. Morris says that lips are a 'genital echo'.

Months before I started dating Aidan, I went to dinner with a friend. We were pretending to be platonic, but there was more simmering away. We often spent weekends sharing a ratty blanket, drinking cheap red wine from coffee cups and watching classics like *Citizen Kane* on his couch, our knees touching, skin prickling with the promise of something that never quite arrived.

At dinner that night in a Vietnamese restaurant close to his house, he waited until I was two bites into a pork spring roll wrapped in lettuce and mint before telling me the deep red Seven Deadly Sins lipstick that I was wearing was particularly attractive because the colour mimicked my labia.

I nearly choked.

Even now, I can feel the flush of heat in my cheeks and the flustered attempt to concentrate on the plate of phallic-shaped food between us. The promise of intimacy ended with his comment. Instead of making me want him, it made me feel out of my depth, as if I was still practising at being a woman.

I searched for a comeback, something witty and sophisticated. But I found nothing. And returned to eating my spring roll, shoving it all into my mouth so there would be no need to speak.

★

Act Two: Death

Aidan's lips were like a letterbox. He used to joke about them. 'Thin as a pencil,' he'd say.

My first real kiss was with a boy we called Bowl because his mother used one regularly to cut his hair. I was fourteen and we were at a train station late on a Saturday afternoon. Even then, outer-suburban train stations were not considered romantic. They were covered in graffiti, fights used to erupt regularly, and you'd never want to be alone at the station at night.

I had no feelings for Bowl, but he was the odd one out like I was. We were the only two not matched in our group. I think we probably thought *better than nothing*.

Kissing was sort of an obsession during high school, made worse by the fact that I was on the outer of most of it. I had crushes, improper ones on teachers and boys already taken. When my friend wanted to kiss a girl, he rang me and I told him to find a pillow and practise while we talked. I passed myself off as some sort of expert when I was more inexperienced than him.

Back then I'd clock up time on the home phone, stretching the cord as far as I could before it pulled out of the jack. Sometimes a parent would pick up the extension phone and tell me to get off. But mostly I spent hours lying on the floor, feet up the wall trying to be as cool as Molly Ringwald, dishing out relationship advice like I was indispensable.

For our only kiss, Bowl and I stood as far apart as possible on the edges of the station car park, leaning forward so just our lips would touch. The kiss was fast and lacking passion because my friend's father was waiting in the car, impatiently tooting the horn, making it clear he wanted to leave before someone parked him in.

It was not the first kiss described in the *Sweet Dreams* books that I'd read or like the first kiss my best friend had shared with a boy two years older. It was a kiss that I would happily forget if I could.

After Bowl, in my red vinyl-covered teenage diary I wrote that the boy I would marry would be the first I kissed using my tongue. I was naïve, a bookish kid stuck in the romances of pages and not of real life. I had a painful crush on the actor Tom Selleck in his role as Magnum, P.I., with small newspaper pictures of his face lining my bookshelves. Looking back, I don't know why. Maybe it was his moustache, maybe it was his detective work or maybe it was because he was older and he fitted a trope that I had constructed.

Years later, I remember being delighted by an episode of *Friends* when Monica dates Tom Selleck's character, Dr Richard Burke, an ophthalmologist old enough to be her father. I'd stopped finding him attractive by then but was thrilled by the thought that perhaps someone in the casting department had experienced the same crush as me, way back when, and had rolled out the slightly older-looking Tom Selleck, complete with the same moustache, as a love interest.

Under the single bed in my childhood bedroom, I also kept a box of newspaper clippings on Swedish tennis star Stefan Edberg. The pencil hearts I'd drawn around Stefan's signed name in my ratty autograph book revealed my feelings. My younger brother discovered it one day and teased me for hours. I was mortified that he'd discovered my secret love.

Act Two: Death

Each year from the age of nine to fifteen, I'd turn up every summer to Kooyong Lawn Tennis Club to watch the Australian Open tennis tournaments and hang around the practice courts outside, waiting for the big-name players to arrive. I was dressed in eighties pastels, with my long fair hair pulled back in a ponytail. Channelling the detective work that I'd learnt from watching *Magnum, P.I.*, I'd wait for someone to wander past in a white tracksuit, carrying a bag full of racquets slung over their shoulder, and then shove my autograph book into their hands with a pen.

I found the autograph book when the kids and I moved house after Aidan died. Under each tennis star's illegible scrawl, I've written their name in neat pencil letters. They are all in there: Martina Navratilova, Pam Shriver, Mats Wilander.

Dad is in the book too: *To Nuff, my darling daughter and dancing partner.*

And friends who must have invented signatures just to fill the coloured pages at the front.

Now, the spine of the book is cracked and the pages are loose, but I can still feel the buzz of my teenage heart as I watched a tennis star hunch over to scribble their name.

I played competitive tennis three times a week until I grew boobs and was too embarrassed to wear a bra. I developed earlier than my friends and discovered that Mum was discussing my body with some of the other mothers. I hid my shape in clothes baggy enough for three of me but still Mum wanted to drag me off to be fitted in a department store.

Desperate to avoid some older woman's cold fingers on my

skin, I used to pull my singlet down as tight as I could and tuck it into a pair of elastic bloomers, trying to flatten my chest. The fear of this must have stayed with me because I wrote about it years later in my middle-grade novel *Sick Bay*, where the character of Riley has to endure a change-room scene for her first bra fitting with her mum.

Flattening my chest didn't work. My boobs kept growing. And they were noticed. The boys at high school stood in a long line and rated our chests, holding up scorecards they'd made themselves. A girl they nicknamed 'Big-ones' came first. I came second and was handed a plastic pair of breasts, large enough to wear, as my trophy.

I hated the feeling of my boobs wobbling as I ran, so I stopped tennis and hung up my racquet, surrendering my love of the Swedes and finding a crush much closer to home.

The farmer's son wasn't famous and he wasn't a character in a TV series. He had blond hair and olive skin and looked like a model in *Dolly* magazine. He was the first real boy I imagined kissing and I wrote about it often in my diary. Our meeting place – not that he knew it – was the mobile library van.

His younger brother had been in my class at primary school; he was a compulsive liar, inventing gruesome injuries that caused him to limp or use his other hand to write. I don't remember when I found out that his stories weren't true. Perhaps Mum told me later, or perhaps I had a nose for liars, even then. But at some point, when I decided I wanted to be like Agatha Christie, I became more intrigued about why he lied rather than about the lies themselves. Sometimes I would try to trip him up with teenage logic but it never worked. He had the ultimate poker face.

Act Two: Death

I was taken with the farmer's son for years and would hide down the back of the children's section in the mobile library van, watching him at the other end, browsing books in his grey woollen blazer with dark grey shorts and long white socks pulled to his knees. I went to the local high school and wore a shapeless checked blue, red and white dress that I sometimes belted with my itchy blue woollen jumper so more of my legs could be seen.

As an adult I learnt that he had been writing love letters to my mum the whole time I'd been mooning over him. He would leave them on the windscreen of her car when she picked me up from school. After Mum died, her friend told me and we giggled about it but, somewhere inside, my teenage heart was injured.

Mum knew I liked him but she never even hinted at the letters that he and his friend wrote to her. I think she kept that secret because she didn't want to hurt me.

Now in my early fifties and single, I do not like reading in Kirshenbaum's book that women's lips are at their fullest when they reach puberty and their thinnest after menopause, and that perhaps this is a signal to a mate when a woman is at her most fertile. It makes me feel overcooked, past my use-by date, no longer worthy of attraction.

I prefer concentrating on the scientific offering that most of us spend about two weeks kissing in our lifetimes. That is over twenty thousand minutes of kissing. Maybe that means I still have some time left. Although how that has been researched is less clear.

Aidan didn't live to be an average age. We did not get to grow old together. He died days before I turned fifty, when he was fifty-three. I hope he kissed enough during his kissing years to make up for the fact that he died early.

I can picture him writing – left-handed, leaning deep across the page, his elbow smudging his writing as he moved, making his words blurry sometimes. But I don't remember which way Aidan tilted his head when we kissed.

I do remember that our kissing stopped when he was diagnosed. Intimacy became something more comforting, like a reassuring hug. We didn't talk about not kissing, we just stopped. He was sad. And I was lost.

I'd always loved kissing Aidan. And to lose that at the time when you are aware you are going to lose the person too was hard. To raise it with him felt unfair. He was already apologetic about his cancer, like he blamed himself for it upending our lives.

During his treatment, he was referred to the dentist at the cancer hospital. He'd always smiled in a particular way so the camera didn't seek out his bad teeth. Some were rotten and removed, others with cavities and filled. He was sensitive about them, embarrassed even.

And then the dentist told him they had to all come out. 'The Hulk' treatment Aidan was starting on made him at risk of mouth sores, infections and teeth decay from the changes caused by chemotherapy and radiotherapy in the lining of the mouth and salivary glands.

That day he came home from the hospital changed. He could cope with the nerve damage of chemotherapy, the dry mouth, the ulcers, the loss of muscle and body hair, but to be told his teeth were going to be removed was something else.

Act Two: Death

I wanted Aidan to see another dentist and ask if removing his teeth was the best option. But he was overwhelmed by the prognosis, the treatment and the endless appointments. Under local anaesthetic, he had most of his top teeth removed. They left several at the front so that if he smiled it wouldn't look too obvious.

He never smiled properly again.

When he returned to have a check-up, the other dentist admitted she didn't think it had been necessary and nobody seemed to remember that he was supposed to have the bottom row removed too.

In my teenage diary, I wrote that *kissing with tongues is gross*. I now know that male saliva contains testosterone and a few molecules of testosterone will raise a woman's libido, presumably making it more likely that it won't stop at just a kiss. Aidan was having injections to block his testosterone so perhaps he knew instinctively there was no point trading saliva.

I remember our last kiss. It was a few days before he died. We'd argued playfully about him wanting me to make yet another pot of coffee. Even when he stopped eating, he still drank cup after cup of coffee and half of my day was spent running the stairs to deliver him one.

Years back, when I'd worried that he drank too much caffeine, I'd started buying decaffeinated coffee and filling the old metal canister with it. I justified this lie as being good for him, but when he started feeling jittery and detached from things, I had to confess. He was understandably angry.

That day when I acquiesced and delivered him another coffee, with a rubber straw sticking from the top of the cup, he told me he loved me and I bent down and touched my lips to his.

There's a kissing scene in the independent American film *Lars and the Real Girl*, which Aidan and I watched a month or so after one of his brothers died. In the film, Ryan Gosling plays Lars, a man who can barely stand being touched by another person. His parents are dead and he avoids people as often as he can. One day he orders a life-sized vinyl doll on the internet. Her name is Bianca and he takes her everywhere with him: to the shops, to church, to dinner at his brother's place. At first people are horrified that Lars seemingly treats Bianca as if she is real, but over time everyone in the town starts to accept her too because she makes Lars happy and that is enough.

In this scene, Lars leans close and kisses Bianca on the mouth. As he pulls away, he starts to cry. In that moment, we forget we are watching a life-sized doll being kissed by a man. Because Lars loves Bianca and believes she is real, we are moved.

There are so many ways this film could have gone wrong. Only it doesn't. It's tender and raw and a rare examination of the complexity of mental illness.

It's one of the few films Aidan and I watched without comment. By the end he was sobbing, hands clutched over his face and incapable of speech. I'd never seen Aidan cry like this and my attempts at comforting him failed.

He just kept crying.

Even now, I'm not entirely sure why. Whether he saw himself

in the slightly removed character of Lars, or if it was a ripping open of grief for his brother, or if it was something else. Something basic and human.

But when Aidan was dying, lying in a t-shirt with bare legs because it hurt having pyjama pants inched up over his skin, I was reminded of the loneliness that Lars had felt. Aidan seemed so far away from all that he was, like a man watching the world pass by, knowing he would never re-enter it.

And when I kissed him on the mouth that day, that final time, it wasn't a kiss of passion, but of farewell.

Scene Six: Goodbyes

I've always been terrible at goodbyes. I'll slowly circle the room at a party, never one to slip away without kissing each cheek or hugging each person in farewell. Aidan was a 'party, then leave' sort of person. Once he'd decided he'd had enough, he'd walk out. Sometimes that meant he was waiting for me outside as I made fresh plans or promised to catch-up, traded numbers, declared friendship. Sometimes it meant he'd whisper that he'd see me at home because it was clear my lap of goodbyes wasn't goodbye at all, but in fact more late-night hellos.

Even when he was dying, it was on his terms. When it's my turn, I fear I'll be so busy having conversations I'll forget to draw inward and prepare.

★

Act Two: Death

When my mum was dying, she made it clear she didn't want many visitors to the palliative care ward. Just us, a couple of close friends, her children, their partners and her husband. That was it.

I made the decision to bring my children in to say goodbye. They were close to her, loved her like a third parent. My daughter was turning eight and had just chopped her hair short in a sort of rockabilly do. I remember Mum clutching her hand and telling her it 'suits you'. Then Mum looked up at me, furious that I'd ignored her request. Having them there was just too much life leaking into her room.

When Aidan was dying, Covid meant that we didn't really get to choose whether we saw people or not. Mostly it was just the four of us in our ugly rented townhouse, with the only regular visitor being a nurse twice a week for an hour each time. Friends relied on me for updates so I would send out occasional emails telling them how sick Aidan was.

In late August 2020, we had a telehealth appointment with an oncologist. Aidan and I were sitting on the edge of the hired hospital bed in our bedroom. He was in pyjamas. I probably was too. It wasn't with our usual oncologist, the one we'd had since the beginning. He'd vanished now that Aidan was too sick to help. We had someone new. She was kind and respectful, gently explaining things via the screen of the laptop.

It was hard to find information and have questions answered during lockdowns. There were no incidental meetings with medical staff or opportunities for me to ask discreet questions away from Aidan. We had to do it via a screen.

And that day, I asked her the question.

'How long?'

It's a question that is always asked so poignantly in books and films, and yet in real life it's so prosaic.

The oncologist checked with Aidan to see if he wanted to know, like perhaps I'd spoken out of turn. And perhaps I had. I hadn't pre-warned Aidan that I was going to ask the question, it just bubbled up.

Aidan nodded.

I remember her clearing her throat before she answered.

'Maybe weeks.'

Aidan gripped my hand. He seemed surprised, which surprised me.

Afterwards, we kept talking with her about practical things: medications, pain relief, the possibility he would lose full function of his legs and what that would mean for nursing in the home when we lived in a place with so many stairs.

Then the oncologist ended the appointment and the screen went black.

We both started sobbing.

Final days. End of life. Dying. It didn't matter how we phrased it, the outcome was the same. I updated all our friends and family. And then I went down the street and spent too much money on a Nintendo Switch and two games: *The Legend of Zelda* and *Mario Kart*. I was looking for anything that would elevate the mood, that would distract from what was really happening.

The kids had played before at other people's houses but, until then, the only video game console we'd owned was an ancient thing that I'd found cheap at a garage sale. It had been played once

Act Two: Death

and then used as a doorstop. As a child I had a Game Boy and knew how to climb the ladders in *Donkey Kong* and outrun the ghosts in *Pac-Man*, but I didn't play games as an adult. Not since Aidan and I almost broke up when we became jointly obsessed with *Tetris* in 1998 and began dreaming in sequences of falling blocks, fighting constantly over whose turn it was next.

The kids were shocked when they unwrapped the Nintendo Switch. I didn't explain that it was a softening for the recent news, but they knew. They understood the currency. They understood that their dad was dying and they were being given a video game by their mum who didn't know what else to do.

Within days, we each had our *Zelda* routines and none of us approached the game in the same way. My son was desperate to complete the quest first. My daughter was methodical, hunting down each temple to complete before moving on. I just wanted to kill the Moblins. Once I figured out how to use my weapons, I would return to the same site over and over again, slaying as many Moblins as I could, with little interest in proceeding any further.

The game filled time. It gave us something to do while we were waiting. Waiting for lockdowns to end, waiting for restrictions to ease and, ultimately, waiting for Aidan to die.

The Legend of Zelda is a quest game where you become the character of the young protagonist Link who must undertake multiple steps to achieve the goal of saving the magical land of Hyrule from the evil Ganon. Personally, I have little interest in understanding the backstory or completing any stage of the quest. My interest lies only in swinging a sword and firing a bow.

In this game, like in many others, you can die often and you can die spectacularly. You can die when you're too cold, when you lose a battle with a creature, when you drown, when you fall from a height too great, when you're electrocuted, when you burn, when you're crushed by a rock. You can even die being headbutted over a cliff by a goat. There are apparently more than one hundred ways to die when playing *Zelda* and there are entire fan sites dedicated to celebrating the most absurd ones.

And like all video games, each time you die, you can come back to life. It may cost you to do this, depending on the game, but you can always keep playing. In *Zelda*, there is an autosave if you forget to manually save your progress, so that even after you die you are never too far from your last save. You have multiple hearts in the game and can restore them by eating various foods.

Death as a philosophical concept in video games has been written about many times and for anyone who is a regular player, something you have probably considered.

As a game novice, I had not.

It is only now that I look back on our playing at that time, when I introduced a way of dying daily into a house where we were caring for someone who *was* actually dying, that I have tried to understand the philosophy more. Perhaps the elation I felt at shooting the Moblins with my found arrows and watching them flare and disappear was my way of feeling in control. Just like reading crime novels or watching television shows where people are brutally murdered, this was another way of dancing around death without it being too real or overwhelming.

Or perhaps it was just fun. A true moment of distraction.

I cannot play *Zelda* now. It reminds me too much of this time.

★

Act Two: Death

Aidan had a go at the Nintendo Switch, but he wasn't invested. Instead, as a distraction, he made a list of the people he loved. Unlike Mum wanting to keep everyone away, Aidan decided that it was time to allow those closest to him to come and say goodbye. Just like when he monitored the endless stream of visitors in the early weeks after our daughter was born, it was now my turn to become the gatekeeper to our lives.

For months we'd obeyed the restrictions of the pandemic and because Aidan had been too unwell to get down the stairs and go outside for an hour of exercise each day, he hadn't really seen anyone. Even his closest friends hadn't watched the debilitating progression of his cancer. When one of them saw him after several months of restrictive lockdowns, she cried at the sight of his slow shuffle and had to hide her face so he wouldn't witness her shock.

We decided to go against restrictions and open our house to visitors for a week. I emailed a small group of family and friends and explained that they'd have to be tested and isolate until it was their turn to visit. It was still taking up to a week for Covid-test results to come back at this stage, so isolating meant some of our friends couldn't work. They also had to lie to various testing facilities, pretending they had a sore throat or a headache, because Covid tests were not readily available then unless you had symptoms.

I made a roster of days and times, scheduling multiple visitors across each day, and converted our former bedroom into a hospital room. For seven days, we filled the house with cakes and flowers and conversation. Masks were worn, sanitiser was used, letters of love and friendship were left on the food tray table.

Aidan had spent most of the previous weeks sleeping and chatting to me or the kids, maybe watching a bit of telly from his bed. Now he talked and laughed and held court in a way that I hadn't seen him do since before he was diagnosed. He was present. The pain and the sadness and the fear were on hold.

It was a week like nothing I've experienced.

A week of goodbyes.

Some people came alone. Others in groups. One friend brought her twin twelve-year-old sons to say goodbye and they joked about stuff as if he was going to be fine. One friend made a chocolate cake and Aidan managed a few bites. Another arrived with KFC in a bucket and they picked at fried chicken. Someone sitting near Aidan's bed realised the windows were dirty outside and came back with a ladder and a bucket to clean them, knowing that he would have hated looking out through the grimy glass.

All the time, I hovered, sometimes in the doorway, or pulling up a chair, or hiding out upstairs in the kitchen making coffee. I didn't want it to be about me. And I also didn't want to watch. Watching him like this was harder than seeing him silent and grey. It kept tugging me back to before. When he was well and sharp. When he was strong and able. When he was funny and erudite.

The most crushing visits for me to watch were those with his male friends the same age. They traded jokes and stories, remembering things from before, and laughed in their familiar way. I can't imagine how it felt for them either. Particularly as they hadn't seen him slowly fade as I had. It must have been brutal.

Until cancer, Aidan had always been in his body. Physically capable, with cuts and nicks on the back of his hands from fixing something or other. And now he was relying on me to hand him his medication and bring him a drink, holding it up to his lips so he could sip through a straw.

By the end of that week, he was spent. He couldn't face another visit. He was done. I was too. And our house settled back into the quiet of online schooling, the regular interruption of *Zelda* and the mechanical hum of his hospital bed.

Scene Seven:
And the Light Goes Out

Genetically, there are times during the day where we are most productive, most alert, when the heart is most efficient and when our blood pressure is highest. Our innate body clock determines if we are a night owl or an early riser, and scientific research suggests that not only do circadian rhythms dictate when we wake each day, but quite possibly the time of day that we will die.

And according to a number of articles that come up when you google, most people die around eleven am.

My mum died at four am when we were six coffees in and on constant watch, listening for the rattle of her final breaths.

But not Aidan.

He'd stopped speaking on the Friday afternoon. His dear friend and theatre collaborator had dropped in for his second farewell and Aidan had asked for a soft drink. I held the can, offered him the plastic bendy straw, but wouldn't let him hold it because I'd already mopped up and changed him three times that week when he'd dropped coffee and drinks. It wasn't easy manoeuvring him into new clothes or changing sheets. It meant a tablet of breakthrough oxycodone to mask the pain, and then carefully sliding the fabric under him, around him, over him, to avoid upsetting his position.

That day, when I kept my hand firmly on the can, he looked up at me with a loose throwaway smile and said lightly, 'Get fucked, Nov.' He was showing off one last time. Being the Aidan we both longed to see. We both laughed, like the good audience, but inside I just wanted him to keep the fight.

On the Friday, he whispered that he loved me but there was no big declaration of meaning or goodbye. It was, as it had always been, Aidan inching slowly away and neither of us quite accepting it.

By Saturday, his breathing was ragged and his mouth gaped as if the muscles had stopped doing their job. He was sweaty and still. If I tried to move him, he'd grimace like the pain was too much. Our children avoided the room, skirting around it and disappearing outside to walk with friends.

I sensed it was getting closer.

But the nurse didn't think death would come for another few days. Just in case, that night I slept on the floor alongside his bed, and drifted in and out of strange dreams and thoughts, worried that I'd miss his last breaths.

On Sunday morning, the nurse dropped in to replenish the morphine vials and to help me turn Aidan so that he was more comfortable. During those hours, one of his sisters and two of his oldest friends arrived, each needing to see him one last time.

I think about these visits sometimes. My lack of care for those grieving him. How I was so trapped in the moment to moment of my fragile day that I could barely consider crying or feeling. How often I wanted the world to leave us, so I could keep him all to myself.

But those visitors, those friends and family, they were the ones bringing in the tears and the heartfelt confessions. They were the ones gripping his hand and declaring their feelings. I was too preoccupied with making him coffees, feeding him sandwiches, changing his clothes when he sweated through t-shirt after t-shirt. I didn't have time for sitting by his bed saying words of comfort because I was phoning doctors, negotiating for scripts to be sent to the chemist, arranging for someone to collect medications, taking him to the toilet, and worrying, always worrying, about what came next. I'd stopped being his lover and started being his nurse. And I was so jealous of anyone who could just *be*.

After the real nurse left on that Sunday morning, my son went to rollerskate in the car park down the road. His friend was meeting him for a treasure hunt, organised by her mum to provide my son with some small moment of joy in his bleak days.

I'd arranged for one of Aidan's besties, Barb, to come over. Before running restaurants, she'd trained as a nurse and wasn't afraid of what was coming. Our daughter was floating around, not really committing to being anywhere, but knowing that she didn't want to leave. I was booked to do an hour-long author session on Zoom for a literary festival that had 'pivoted' online. Since Aidan had become bedbound, I'd delayed or surrendered most of my work, but this felt doable. Barb was going to sit with

Act Two: Death

him and hold his hand while I did the online session upstairs. It was a paid gig and it was something other than the routine of my days, something that represented my old world.

I'm not sure now why I held so tightly to the idea that I could do it. I think perhaps I didn't want to believe that Aidan was ready to go, so I just kept ploughing on. It seems so ludicrous that I didn't cancel, that I thought my mind would be steady enough to make me worth watching.

I've lost count of the times that people have called me strong. While Aidan was dying it was the thing I heard more than anything else. I'm not sure that strength is my most-played hand. I think it's probably denial or the ability to split difficult thoughts from the rest of my working day. I've always been very good at resetting each morning, pressing that button and wiping the old away.

It doesn't make me strong. I'm just terrible at showing weakness. I hide vulnerability. I rarely cry around anyone, saving it all for when I go driving. And I power on like the sheer determination of meeting each day will mean things will work out. It's a strategy that leaves me flailing sometimes. It's the reason I thought I could keep working while looking after Aidan. It's the reason I thought I didn't need help to care for him. It's the reason that now when I see people on the street, I can make small talk and appear like my life is fine.

That Sunday afternoon, Barb made doughnuts, or at least I think she did. It's hazy. I still have the moulds in my cupboard with the hole cut out and the small box of pre-mixed cinnamon and sugar she carried with her from home in case we didn't have any. I don't remember if I ate a doughnut or if in fact they were even cooked. But afterwards, we laughed because we couldn't believe that doughnuts were our focus for a time.

I left Barb with Aidan. She placed a sleeping mask over his eyes because they drooped and stared, and she thought it would be nicer for him and us. She turned on music – played Morrissey and The Smiths on his laptop – all his old favourites. She rubbed his feet with special cream.

And I went upstairs to say hello to the other panellists on Zoom and arrange my screen so the light was just right. It was the first time I'd brushed my hair in weeks. I'd even put on lipstick. I didn't look like me.

It was a minute before three pm and the organisers were letting people into the session.

Barb yelled out from downstairs.

I ran.

Left the screen open.

Screamed for my daughter.

We met by Aidan's bed.

Held his hand.

He took his last two quiet breaths.

And was gone.

Three o'clock on a sunny September Sunday.

'There Is a Light That Never Goes Out' by The Smiths was playing on Aidan's laptop.

Barb crept up the stairs and couldn't work out how to log out of the now-happening Zoom panel. She gave them an apologetic wave and closed the screen.

Act Two: Death

Later, I noticed that a close friend had texted me to see if everything was okay. She was watching, saw me run out of the room from the screen.

Barb went to find our son in the car park.

He came home, crumpled on the stairs, his rollerskates demanding their own step, his grey helmet still tight on his little head.

I swallowed him up with tears and arms.

Our daughter refused to leave Aidan's side.

Barb was there.

We cried.

I tried to coax our daughter out of the room, remembering how I felt after Mum died. Our daughter wouldn't come.

I ran back to our son who wasn't ready to go in.

I ran back to our daughter who didn't want to leave.

The nurse arrived and took away the catheter. She gave me paperwork. She couldn't hug me because of Covid. But her eyes were warm.

Barb helped me text and let people know.

I drank whiskey in fast noisy gulps.

Barb rang the funeral home and arranged for Aidan's body to be collected in a couple of hours.

Our daughter finally let herself leave.

We all sat on the step, squashed together, crying in the afternoon sun.

After Barb left, the kids huddled on my daughter's bed with her guitar. She played Morrissey songs and sang, loud and true.

I snuck into the bedroom. Sat with Aidan. Dressed him in pyjamas.

Barb left boxes of tissues on the doorstep and afterwards told me she could hear the wailing sobs from outside on the street and my daughter's voice singing.

I snipped strands of Aidan's soft grey hair and tucked it in my drawer. I waited for the men with the truck to come and take his body.

Upstairs my kids watched *Gilmore Girls* and ate pizza that a friend had delivered. I drank more whiskey and wanted Aidan gone. But didn't.

The men arrived. One was tall and stooped, a little like the English actor Stephen Merchant. He stepped inside in a suit and bent down and hugged me. He apologised because of Covid but hugged me anyway and my arms wouldn't work so I was braced and awkward.

They explained what would happen. How they'd wrap Aidan in fabric and take him downstairs and drive him to the funeral home in the country.

I left them to it.

And checked on the kids.

They were staring at the screen.

I followed Aidan on the gurney downstairs to the front door. Stopped our cat from escaping. Stephen Merchant checked that the street was clear. It wasn't.

They had to wait for a man walking his dog to pass. I thought that I'd never considered how upsetting it might be to see a body carried from a suburban house.

They took Aidan out and whispered goodbye to me. I shut the door. It was night.

I stared into the room where Aidan had died. The pump was

Act Two: Death

still plugged in on the air-inflating mattress. I crept underneath the hospital bed and turned it off at the wall. I pulled the curtain, not wanting the world to wake up to him being gone. Not yet.

I went upstairs.

Nuzzled between my children. Poured another whiskey. Watched the final episode of *Gilmore Girls*. And cried.

Interval Two:
Untitled

Deciding on a title for this book without you is hard. Historically, you are the person I would be asking. And you would wait until the kids were out and then you'd make a pot of coffee, maybe fry some eggs and we'd sit down at the kitchen table and talk. You'd have music playing and I'd ask if I could turn it off because it's impossible for me to think with Cat Power singing over me. You'd jump up and take care of it, knowing that if I did, there was a fair chance I wouldn't put the record back in the sleeve and it would collect dust.

While you were away from the table, I'd steal the crust from your plate and maybe swipe a little piece of egg too, and you'd pretend to be frustrated and offer again to make me my own serve, which I'd refuse before eating more of yours.

Then, as you drink your coffee and eat more of your eggs, cutting the bread in your heavy left-handed way, I'd list all the title options and you'd nod, considering each one before dismissing it as not quite right until the list is no more. I'd start to panic and you'd let me for a minute or two, and then suggest a different one that I hadn't thought of, one that wrapped around the pages of the story and held them tight, one that said everything it needed to say.

And I'd kiss you and tell you how amazing you are. And you'd laugh but also accept the praise. Or maybe you'd even make a joke that, yes, you are amazing. And then I'd move on to all the other moments in the book that I'm unsure of and ask your opinion.

You'd listen while you finished your food and then you'd clean up while we talked. You'd stack the dishwasher, soak the pan, make another pot of coffee, maybe even wipe down the table if crumbs had escaped your breakfast plate. And just when I'd given up on thinking you were going to help me, you'd tell me what you thought, and I'd hang on every word, knowing you'd solve it, you'd crack the case. And you did. Every time.

Without you, I'm writing in the dark.

Act Three:
Other Scenes

Scene One:
No Time for Rituals

Until I had to organise for Aidan's body to be removed from our house, I hadn't thought much about funerals or their history. But afterwards, I read all the books on grief and death and mourning that I could find. I disappeared down a research hole. I think I was hunting out company, wanting to know that what I felt had already been experienced by others. Mostly, I wanted to feel less alone.

Somewhere among the memoirs and the personal stories, I started reading a book called *In the Midst of Life* by Des Tobin and Graeme M Griffin. I learnt that until the First World War, Christian funerals in this country were largely a home affair. Hospitals were not keen on taking patients who would likely die because it would upset their ability to raise funds. Instead, the body would be laid out at home, dressed and prepared for the vigil. Unsurprisingly, women organised and ran the funeral service.

And largely because of religion, death was considered something beautiful and transitional, the release of the spirit to heaven.

Things changed with the number of soldier deaths during the war and then the mass deaths during the flu pandemic, and funerals shifted away from the home to a professional service. Tobin and Griffin explain that this was due to high anxiety in the community about death and an attempt to avoid all reminders of it. And when crematoriums were built after the First World War, the funeral industry changed again.

Aidan wanted to die at home. And we both knew that if he went into palliative care then the kids wouldn't be allowed to see him due to Covid restrictions. I'm not sure what decision we would have made had there been no pandemic, but he'd always hated hospitals and he liked the comfort and the closeness of having us around him.

I learnt about funeral etiquette from watching Aidan. He had a dark second-hand suit hanging in the cupboard ready to go when needed. Sometimes he spoke the eulogies, other times he helped to write the words. If we were in a church, he always knew when to stand, when to amen and when to cry. He was practised at it.

There was no formal funeral for Aidan. No coming together to mourn. The day he was cremated was gloomy and grey and it happened miles away from our home. Melbourne was still in lockdown and funerals were limited to only eight guests. The kids and I couldn't imagine who we'd invite, so we decided we'd wait and hold a memorial later when all our friends and family could come together to celebrate his life.

Act Three: Other Scenes

After his body was taken from our house, he was driven to the funeral home that was the least like a funeral home I could find. A friend had rung around to find somewhere that was low-key and offered environmentally sustainable shrouds without costing too much. The place she found was in regional Victoria. If none of us could leave Melbourne because of Covid lockdown, at least Aidan could.

The funeral director rang me to see if I wanted to say goodbye to him before cremation. I hadn't planned on going because I thought I'd already said everything I had to say but, as I was talking to her, I realised that some family members had arranged to sit with him, and it mattered that I was the last person to kiss him goodbye. The funeral director explained that it is more common than you'd imagine that a partner wants to say the final farewell.

We had to apply for official permission to cross into regional Victoria to farewell Aidan at the funeral home. We had to present the documentation to the police as we crawled off the highway and through the roadblock that had been set up as a 'ring of steel' around metropolitan Melbourne. The policeman scanned the paperwork, checked my driver's licence and waved us through. We hadn't ventured outside our permitted five-kilometre zone in months, and now we were on the other side of the roadblock in a regional town without restrictions.

The kids decided they didn't want to see their dad. They'd already said their goodbyes on the day he died. I understood. Part of me didn't want to go in either. I told them I'd come and find them in an hour or two and dropped them in the main street with my credit card. The op shops were all open and they hadn't shopped for months because Melbourne was still closed.

I drove to the funeral home that looked more like a display home for a new housing estate than anything housing the dead. I parked in a visitor's spot and tucked a tissue into my sleeve. Only one tissue, like I thought that would be enough.

The funeral director showed me through and told me to take as long as I liked. The air inside the room was chilled and I knew it was for Aidan, so that he remained the right temperature. I pulled my cardigan tighter and looked everywhere but at him.

When Mum had died in the early morning, I'd left the room as quickly as I could because I couldn't make sense of her not breathing. I'd helped Dad pick out clothes for her to wear for cremation but had no need to see her in them.

And now here I was in a small room with my dead partner lying on the bed in front of me. He looked waxy and I touched his skin, thinking perhaps that it would still give, like it did just after he died. But it was solid. And cold.

It was a long time since I'd seen him dressed in anything but pyjamas. He looked more like him than he had when he was dying. He was dressed in the clothes I'd left out: a grey linen shirt, dark pants he sometimes wore, and slip-on Birkenstocks that needed a polish. They'd clipped a goatee and had washed his silvery hair. It was soft and flyaway like it had never been before. It was the only thing that moved. There was no product in it, fixing it into his trademark quiff.

I tried to sit down in the chair to the right. I reached for his hand, but I didn't like how it felt. I found myself wondering how they'd chosen an expression for his face. He looked slightly amused and it suited him.

Act Three: Other Scenes

I tried talking to him. Then felt ridiculous. He wasn't there, but he was.

I stayed for as long as I could. Over an hour. I felt guilty wanting to leave. I cried more than once, using up the tissue I'd brought with me in a second and then half the box provided.

Before I left, I kissed his forehead and tucked a note into his pocket that the kids had written him. I told him how we loved him. I kept imagining that he would respond, that he was somewhere watching and he'd catch up to me and we'd talk. Unpack all that had happened. I knew he'd have things to say on the matter, make me see it differently.

The funeral director walked me to the car. She was kind and let me lead. I obviously didn't want to talk. I was still crying when I backed the car out slowly, onto the side street. It was a cool day, but I felt uncomfortable in my cardigan, like it was too restrictive. I hadn't worn real clothes for ages. I'd been living in elastic-waisted pants and Aidan's old knitted green jumper the three of us fought over after he died.

At first, I couldn't find the kids on the main street. I drove up and down several times trying to spy them in a window. There was a surge of panic in my chest. Maybe they were gone. Kidnapped. Or murdered. Or they'd run away. Proving that I couldn't keep anyone safe.

On my next lap around the block, I found them swinging bags of stuff between their legs. I parked badly and rushed to them for a hug. They wanted to show me everything they'd bought. They had stories of op-shop security wanting to know where they lived and why they were shopping in regional Victoria.

I said nothing about Aidan, knowing there was nothing to say.

In the back of the car, they had a fashion parade, pulling jumpers and tops over layers of clothes so I could see all the purchases. My daughter had found a cream slip that she loved and my son had bought random stuff, bragging that he'd spent less than her. It was frenzied and unreal, an attempt at restoring the behaviours from when Aidan was still with us.

We went to the pub on the corner for lunch. We were allowed to remove our masks to eat. The threat of Covid had somehow paused for the day.

They ordered excessively, but I wasn't going to rein them in. It was a day to do whatever we needed. We talked about superficial stuff as if Aidan wasn't close by in a fridge. We ate chips and burgers, and I drank a pot of beer as they finished off pints of lemonade. It was like we hadn't eaten in weeks, and we shovelled it all in too fast.

I paid and we walked down the main street looking for a shop that sold icy poles. We found a little health food shop and I bought random things. Locals were filling boxes with vegetables and making small talk and, as I tapped my card on the EFTPOS machine to cover the cost of the shopping, I realised that I would never see Aidan again.

Back in the car I thought that I should return to the funeral home before we drove through the ring of steel. But I knew he'd already be on his way to Bendigo where he'd be cremated in a few hours. I thought he'd be amused about Bendigo because he'd lived there for a few years as a child. He'd attended Gravel Hill Primary School and used to tell us stories of BMX adventures with his friends. His Bendigo years had been happy ones and it seemed fitting that he was returning to that place.

Act Three: Other Scenes

We drove out onto the highway and I tuned the radio to ABC Melbourne. They were doing a dedication to Aidan, talking about him and us. They mentioned the play Aidan wrote based on Tim Rogers & the Twin Set's album *What Rhymes with Cars and Girls*. Aidan and Tim had remained friends and Tim had recorded a Morrissey song for Aidan as a tribute. It was one of Aidan's favourites.

As Tim sang the words to 'This Charming Man' on the radio, I sobbed into the steering wheel. I had to pull off the freeway because I thought I'd crash. I turned into a parking bay near a toilet block. My son reached for my shoulder from the back seat and I tried to bring the three of us together but it was all too much. The kids didn't talk and nothing I said came out the way it should. I was filling gaps, making noise, chattering to try to bridge what we were all feeling. But it didn't work. Tim finished singing and the radio show moved on to something else. I turned it off and pulled back onto the freeway.

I can't remember the rest of the drive home. I can't remember if we ate lollies from the glovebox or stopped for petrol. If we talked or listened to music or travelled silently.

That night at five pm as Aidan's body was cremated in Bendigo, we raised a glass. Friends did the same across the country and sent in photographs to us of faces and sad eyes. There's a shot of the kids and me, with Beanie the cat squashed between us. We're tear-stained and lost, staring up into the flash of the phone, recording the moment that he leaves.

Scene Two: Grief

After Aidan died, our house was groaning with gifts. A carton of freshly laid eggs from someone's chickens, a thermos of negroni to get me through the night, little tins of delicate homemade biscuits with the ingredients listed on the lid. It was a tender blanket of love, arriving only because we were broken, but it helped to read letters, smell flowers and eat handmade chocolates. And at some point, it became a way of lightening the mood.

The doorbell would ring, one of us would hike down three sets of stairs, put a mask on, open the door, accept the parcel, take the mask off and hike back up the stairs. My son started trying to guess what would arrive. Croissants? A bottle of gin? A plant?

One day he opened the door to a delivery person holding a large glass vase full of orchids.

'Flowers for Nora? Congratulations!' the man said to my son as he handed them over.

Act Three: Other Scenes

And for days afterwards, whenever the doorbell rang, we called out to each other, 'Flowers for Nora? Congratulations!'

Presumably the man thought we'd had a new baby, not that someone had just died, but the joy we felt after he left was enormous. And I started referring to myself as Nora. Who knew we'd needed to laugh?

A few days before Aidan's death, the funeral director arrived at our house, wearing a black mask and carrying hand sanitiser. She'd come to talk me through the next steps, and told me that she found water helped move grief through the body. She said it was normal for people to shower more than usual or lie in a bath for hours on end. She told me to drink litres of water to make up for all the tears.

I didn't think much about it at the time. I was too consumed with Aidan's last days to imagine them ever ending. But they did. And when they did, I cried. Sometimes with such force that I couldn't stand.

About a month later, the local pools started reopening. Covid conditions were strict and bookings were almost impossible to get. But a friend told me that she'd heard it wasn't so hard to book at the Carlton Baths because the pool was only twenty-five metres and most of the lap swimmers wanted full-length lanes.

I booked my first swim in many years. It was October. Nearly warm enough for sunscreen. I arrived at the pool several minutes before my allocated fifty. A long line of swimmers already queued down Rathdowne Street. As we slowly shuffled in, masks on, having our temperatures taken, the feeling of being out in a changed world was overwhelming.

I'd forgotten goggles and had to buy some. I slid into the slow lane, joining one other swimmer. We nodded at each other but didn't speak. I hadn't talked to strangers for so long, it didn't seem right to start then.

I let the other swimmer go first, waited until they were almost at the far end before stretching out and kicking off. The water was cool. Three strokes in, I started to cry. I felt held by something bigger, by the force of the water that pressed against me as I lifted my arms and moved down the pool.

I had to pause at the end, to tip the tears from my goggles. I swam until the attendant leant down into my lane and told me my time was up. Nobody could use the change rooms, so I pulled on my clothes, feeling them stick to my wet skin, and carried Aidan's slippers out through reception and into the street.

After that day, I started swimming as often as I could. It helped with the grief. Sometimes it made me cry. Other times it stopped me. Afterwards, my body was so loose from the laps that I came home, lay on my bed and drifted. Swimming emptied me. It took all my anger, all my rage, and spread it across the pool so that it was gone for the day and I could manage the other parts of my life a little easier.

It was also the only time of the day that I didn't think. In those months when grief ebbed around us, being in water meant a break. I wasn't with the kids, I wasn't in the house where Aidan died, I wasn't trying to make money or plan a future; I was just me. Swimming like all the other bodies, nobody watching me to see how I was coping.

★

Act Three: Other Scenes

Those first days after Aidan died were almost euphoric, born from a relief that I didn't have to witness him in pain anymore. The worst had happened. I felt it too after Mum died, driving home at five in the morning when the sun was coming up on the Hoddle Bridge after I'd said goodbye as she took her last breath. I knew I could go home to my kids and just be.

But it's not always that simple, because for months you have cleared all your days for one person, and you don't know when they will stop needing you. Then when they die, particularly if you have cared for them intimately in your home, you suddenly find yourself with too much time. And at first you don't understand how your days are suddenly emptied. It's like bonus time in a video game you didn't even know you were playing.

Because when someone you love is dying, it is everything. If you aren't with them, you're thinking about them. You're becoming an expert on pain relief, medications, healthy eating, hospital navigation, medical speak and worry. You park everything that you need and replace it with thoughts only of them. And it's hard to know how to let yourself back in when they are gone. It's hard to know how to fill that time because of everything else that you are feeling.

All of a sudden, I could shower until the water ran cold. I could sleep without being woken for coffee or drugs. I could leave the house without worrying that he would need me.

When Aidan died, I had so much time.

And with that time, I did what grief asks of us and started looking back to when he was still here.

Grief is not chronological. It does not begin on the day of diagnosis and end on a set date after someone dies. It is random and episodic and it doesn't follow a pattern. Some of us need to talk through our grief, others choose not to. As a society we have constructed a hierarchy to grief. Who has the right to grieve and for how long depends on your perceived relationship with the deceased. As Aidan's partner, my grief was permitted and validated, but I often think about people close to Aidan who had no way of publicly healing because of the isolation of lockdowns, and the lack of an immediate funeral.

With grief comes an audience. The world is watching to see how quickly you recover from your loss. In some cultures, there are rituals to mourning: days spent inside, wearing black, sitting with the body. But for me, grief was a sort of freefall.

According to neuroscientists, our brains can trick us into believing that the dead are returning, forcing us to repeatedly revisit the painful realisation that they are permanently gone. In her book, *The Grieving Brain*, psychologist Mary-Frances O'Connor writes that it's the brain's job to make predictions. This explains why when we first wake up in the morning and our partner of many years is missing from the bed, we do not immediately remember that they are dead because our brains make a calculation based on a lifetime of predictions that they are just in the next room. Because that is where they have been for the previous twenty-five years. And it takes time for our brains to adapt to this new prediction. The brain must play catch-up to the idea that the absence of the person you love is not temporary but permanent. It has to redraw a neural map with this new information.

It is a process of relearning and it hurts.

★

Act Three: Other Scenes

On the days immediately after Aidan died, there was a dangerous looseness to my thinking. I didn't have to consider him anymore.

But I wore his death on my body. In my shoulders that felt tight and sore from having to lift and change him. In my hair that had started to lose its colour and fall out. In my muscles and the vigilant way that they refused to relax.

I saw friends and talked too much. I saw friends and didn't talk enough. I was without a compass and spinning free. I tried to grieve but didn't know how. When I laughed, I felt guilty, like someone would notice and accuse me of not caring. Even now, I can go days without thinking about him and then I'll sense my mood is off, like my nerves are being tickled until they snap, and then I cry.

That first night, the kids and I pulled mattresses into one room so we could be together. Close, touching. I can't remember much of this, only that we slept like that for weeks. And after my new bed arrived, we slept together in that too. There was comfort in the sound of their breathing.

I do remember that first morning after, opening the door to the bedroom where Aidan had died and wanting everything gone: the hospital bed that I'd hired that could raise and lower him with the press of a button; the tray table that slid across his bed where I'd park endless cups of coffee; the commode we silently agreed to largely ignore because of all it represented.

The room had stopped being our shared room when I'd dismantled our queen-sized bed to make space for the hired hospital bed. We'd bought our bed on the cheap twenty years before. It didn't like being dismantled and the shabbily made wooden parts had splintered along the edges as I'd tried. And I'd known as I pulled it apart that I would never sleep alongside Aidan again.

Turning your house into a temporary hospital is both practical and heart-wrenching. It represents a line that you know has been crossed. A no-way-back point. You both understand that when you restore the space to one resembling a bedroom, it will be because the person has died.

As I stood at the doorway and stared in at the room that I'd spent months inside, caring and worrying and loving and crying, I wanted to hurl everything from the window. The scattered chairs where we'd sat watching him sleep, the pump keeping the air mattress moving to prevent bed sores, the plastic tablet box with the days and times marked on the outside, the vases with dying and dead flowers, and the cards written from friends. It had a smell too, of stale air, and the carpet was stained where Aidan had spilt coffee and I hadn't managed to properly mop it up.

I wanted to remember him as more than this.

I'd always assumed that someone would turn up afterwards to collect the vials of morphine, the unopened packets of oxycodone, the jars of steroids, but nobody did. I had an ensuite bathroom stacked full of medications. But nobody came. We had to deal with it.

We filled two rubbish bags with unopened boxes, emptied the morphine vials down the sink, cleared out all the drawers of the twelve different tablets he was taking and my friend took it all away in her people-mover, returning it to the pharmacy to be binned.

The man who had delivered the hospital bed all those weeks ago came back to collect it, and while he was dismantling it we convinced him to take the commode too. It wasn't supposed to be collected because of Covid, but I needed it out.

After the room was cleared, I took the kids to Fitzroy Gardens to escape the sadness that had leached into the house and we sat under a tree near the one that Aidan and I had walked to when I was trying to bring on labour sixteen years before. We didn't talk much. It felt forced and strained, like we had no idea what came next.

Later, we returned home to a clean house, thanks to another friend who'd spent hours scrubbing away the lingering smells of death.

Aidan was gone and now any evidence of his illness was too.

Scene Three: Mourning

Sigmund Freud was the first to write extensively about the processes of grief in his essay *Mourning and Melancholia*. Published in 1917, the essay posits the idea that mourning and melancholia are different responses to the same trigger of loss. Freud argues that mourning is the immediate response to the loss of the person and is the pain of facing the world now that someone you love is no longer there. It is a finite response; as you learn to adjust to them being gone, you move through mourning and into acceptance. But melancholia is the depressive and persistent response to loss, where someone feels their pain internally within their unconscious. The grief gets stuck because the loss is so unbearable that the conscious mind cannot process it and it leads to a depressive state.

I'm summarising a very detailed essay into a takeaway paragraph so I'm not doing it justice, but I take all of this to mean that we need to work through our grief, and if we don't, then I think Freud is saying our grief can become internalised and ultimately lead to depression. Having witnessed what happened to Aidan after losing so many members of his family, and knowing how he believed that the mass of his unattended grief triggered his breakdown, I suspect Freud is on to something.

Years ago, while majoring in psychology at university, I visited the Sigmund Freud Museum in Vienna. I was in my late teens and backpacking around Europe with a friend over the summer break. In my first year of an arts degree, I'd been as precociously obsessed with Freud as I was with Sylvia Plath and I'd wandered through the rooms of the museum, marvelling at the displays. It was all there: Freud's famous bed for psychoanalysis; his daughter Anna Freud's rooms where she too treated patients; their collections of thick, impressive leather-bound books. I still have the full-colour program guide that must have cost me as much as a meal.

Now, I am more interested in the reasons why Freud wrote this essay than I am in understanding all the dense theory. It was written during the First World War, a year before the outbreak of the flu pandemic that killed an estimated fifty million people worldwide, including Freud's daughter Sophie. Perhaps the essay was his version of this book – a way to understand how we grieve, how it changes us and how we can hope to continue after someone we love dies.

Not long after studying Freud, I started working at a cool inner-city arthouse cinema called Cinema Nova. People often assumed I owned the cinema, which I guess meant they thought I was arrogant enough to name it after myself. Sometimes I corrected them and sometimes I didn't, preferring they thought of me as this cashed-up trust-fund kid with great taste in cinema.

My days were spent watching movies in the dark and coming up with inventive ways to publicise them. I was film-obsessed, imagining myself in various glamorous roles as the femme fatale lead, like Uma Thurman's character in *Pulp Fiction*, sporting a sleek black bob and dancing the twist in that white shirt.

It was at Cinema Nova that I first encountered a film that tackled grief from a purely emotional place. Until then, I hadn't considered grieving as anything more than academic.

I was twenty-three when I watched the first of the trilogy of films named for the three colours in the French flag. When I watched this film, I was still years away from dating Aidan. Already in love with him but waiting for him to catch up. Directed by Polish director Krzysztof Kieślowski, the *Three Colours* trilogy were his last films before he died in 1996.

And it was Juliette Binoche in *Three Colours: Blue* who haunted me for many years. The film begins with a car crash on a remote highway, killing a world-famous composer and his young child. Juliette Binoche is the composer's wife and the child's mother, and she is badly injured in the crash but alive.

I haven't seen this film again since it was first released and I struggle to recall much of the story now, except that it is about loss and grief and trying to flee your past. But there is a short scene in the film, or possibly just a sequence, that has always plagued me. In my mind, Juliette Binoche is walking through the Paris streets. She is anguished and she reaches out to run her knuckles along a stone wall. The scene is visceral and raw, and I always imagined Binoche submitting to her art as an actress and scarring her hand with the action.

In interviews Binoche explains that there was a prosthetic hand made for the scene, but it kept falling off, so she told Kieślowski she would scrap the prosthetic and drag her own hand along the wall. Kieślowski was apparently angry with her and refused, which she later said was admirable because she *was* prepared to hurt herself for the film.

Writing about the scene for this book made me want to re-watch it. I couldn't commit to the whole film because I avoid watching women performing grief now, but I did re-watch the scene to test my memory, to see how accurate it was.

The stone wall scene is only twenty seconds long and easy to hunt down. In fact, a simple internet search turns up many theories about the scene, suggesting that others were as taken with it as I was.

As I rewatched it, I was surprised to see that instead of Binoche being surrounded by traffic and noise, she is in fact walking in the quiet of a country road. The background sounds are birdsong and footsteps on gravel. The stone wall is high and you cannot see over it. The camera zooms in on Binoche's face as she walks towards it, one arm carrying a box and the other hand hanging like a dead weight. The second shot tracks along behind her closed fist as she reaches out and drags her knuckles along the wall, the stone cutting her skin until she bleeds. Then, still walking, she pulls her hand away and holds it to her face.

I did not remember this scene accurately at all. In my mind, I had her in a busy Parisian street, walking in the opposite direction, surrounded by people. But while my memory of the detail is inaccurate, my memory of the impact of that scene is correct. I can accept these mismatched memories, knowing how fallible mine are proving to be. So many moments of my life that I should remember are blurry at best, the edges fading and only the emotion remaining.

It is the character's need to end her numbness that haunted me. Her grief demanding that she hurt, so that she feels again. I did not experience this numbness because I watched Aidan slowly fade. I had the privilege, perhaps, of being in the room when it happened, an indisputable fact that forces your mind to begin believing that the person has really gone.

But despite not sharing the character's experience of grief or their desire for pain, there is still something in this scene that speaks to me. The unpredictability of her action, the fearlessness, the need to determine your own experience, even if it's a painful one. And I also understand behaving out of character.

In the film, she has not only lost her lover but her child too, and she is trying to jolt herself back from melancholic depths. At first, she hides away, avoiding people so she can become grief. She is coaxed back out by meeting a man.

I had two children to drag me back. I could not easily succumb to days in bed, forgetting to dress, never feeding myself and surrendering. I still had to do the shopping, clean the toilet, cook dinner. Without them, I'm not sure who I would have been.

Grief is not so filmic when the bins need to go out.

Soon after Aidan died, I had to start writing again because my middle-grade book *The Jammer* was overdue. Each time I opened the word document, I found all I could write about was grief. I fought it for a while, trying hard to create a character who wasn't

Act Three: Other Scenes

feeling all that I was. But finally, I surrendered and accepted that this was the only book that I could write.

My character's mother dies off the page at the beginning of the novel. And the book is the story of how thirteen-year-old Fred deals with her death. It is about found family and the idea of forging new connections when we lose people we love. And it ends with hope on Fred's first Christmas, a little like our own.

I didn't run my knuckles along a stone wall until they bled. I didn't have sex with Aidan's friend. I didn't destroy all his work. But I did sprint into the freezing cold waters of a winter bay in my flimsy bathers. I did walk home late at night alone and slightly drunk. And I did start writing this book too. My own efforts to begin and feel again.

Perhaps grieving gives us licence to behave in unusual ways. For me, it's an experience of being ungrounded, like I'm free to act on a whim. When Mum was staying in the palliative care ward, my brother dropped off some dinner for me because I was doing the night shift. He left me a small bottle of whiskey and, sometime during the night, I drank the lot. I vomited in Mum's ensuite and had to sleep upright in the visitor's chair next to her bed. Those days are hazy now. A blur of carrying her to the toilet, clipping her nails, holding a plastic cup to her mouth for sips of water. But that whiskey moment is clear. It's the last time I was drunk enough to vomit, behaving more like my teenage self than anything resembling an adult.

If Mum had been lucid, I would have admitted my behaviour and she might have rolled her eyes, remembering back to nights where she held back my hair, or picked me up late in the car, or heard the story about the undercooked chicken causing food poisoning. Now, I think I drank the whiskey because I was watching her fade. And perhaps I wanted to numb myself.

The night shift is lonely. You can't text a friend and expect them to answer at three in the morning. You are aware you are watching the person you love die and that each morning brings you that little bit closer.

I couldn't drink whiskey for a while afterwards. The smell still returns me to that ensuite bathroom with the overhead light and the shower she never used because she wasn't strong enough to stand.

Whiskey will always be the drink of grief for me. A traditional choice, particularly at Irish wakes. Neat or on the rocks, it doesn't need accompaniment. It slides down your throat and stops you feeling. Which sometimes is exactly what you need.

Scene Four:
Gone

People often talk about how forgotten they feel after a funeral when the world has moved on but they have not. And it's true that there is a huge drop-off in messages and lasagnes. But for me, the hardest part of the after was in knowing how to casually mention Aidan's death. Because of lockdowns, we'd relied on the information train to share our news, but that meant that not everyone knew. The people in our neighbourhood had not witnessed him deteriorating because we'd all been inside while that happened. So, when we finally emerged from lockdown and re-entered the world without him, his absence needed an explanation.

Aidan had been taking our second-hand cars to a mechanic in Brunswick for years. I'd heard about the mechanic from Aidan, but had never met him. He has glasses and stained-blue overalls and his business is close enough to our house that we can walk home and then back when the car is ready to be collected.

When I drove into the warehouse, the mechanic slid out from under a car. He knew our ageing Subaru, even if he didn't know me. He smiled as he took the keys from me, made a joke about how old the car was looking and then asked me where Aidan was.

For some reason I wasn't ready with an answer.

'He's dead.'

Perhaps I should have dressed it up, but I didn't have the energy anymore, so the words were bare, without any of the usual trimmings we use to prepare someone for such news.

He had questions. I told him the truth. And then he cried. He didn't try to hide it either. There were just a handful of tears that he wiped away with his grease-stained t-shirt before asking me if I was okay.

This was another question I hadn't yet worked out an answer for. I think I might have looked at the ground or scuffed my feet or changed the subject. He read my discomfort and told me about his mother-in-law's recent death and the fact he still missed his dad who died years ago.

We talked about traditions that spring up after someone goes and he admitted to upgrading his father's anniversary toast from his dad's favourite cheap beer to a nicer premium brand. He was thinking of changing the drink that represented his mother-in-law too because he and his wife didn't enjoy the Moscato that she always drank.

We talked about keeping people alive in conversation and memory. We talked for half an hour outside that yard filled with cars, the smell of oil and grease fresh in the air.

As I walked home, forgetting my Covid mask was still on, I cried. Just the usual steady leak of tears that was happening more and more. Mini-encounters like that one were the hardest because usually the person I'd report home to would be Aidan. Now I'll try to tell the kids the story and they'll tune me out halfway through, not really getting the point that I am making. Or perhaps not wanting to see their mother so vulnerable, yet again.

With Aidan missing, I've come to realise that so much of our conversations were about people. Perhaps it was the writer in us both, but we'd often share anecdotes about interactions that we'd had with friends or strangers. He saw people differently from how I did. Broke them down with less emotion and more insight. And I often relied on him to tell me how to deal with a situation.

We were so bound up in each other that I am still not sure where I end without him. We were together most of my adult life and when I think about myself, it is in relation to him. Even our email address is a joining of our names, an odd nod to togetherness during the early stages of our relationship.

Aidan's death has left me with hundreds of hours of unsaid words. My friends kindly tolerate my ranting on various subjects, my need to forensically investigate something that's happened, but it's not the same. I miss the half-finished chats Aidan and I would have while one of us was in the shower. The advice we'd impart on the fly. His text messages reminding me to buy milk.

Nobody reminds me to buy milk anymore. I'm just supposed to remember.

With Aidan gone, I long for a witness. Someone to share moments with. I try to spread them around my friends, not wanting to overload anyone for fear of becoming needy.

I worry that I'm disappearing, becoming a person who never fully tells the truth. One night my daughter tells me to stop talking to her like she is my partner. She doesn't want to know.

She's right to reject this. But still it hurts.

People ask me if I'm okay. I appreciate the question but understand that mostly they don't want all the details. They don't want to know about the nights I wake, jaw locked, head pounding, not being able to breathe. That's going to kill a conversation right there.

With him gone, I listen for his boot stamps on the floor late at night when he'd try to creep in from a trip to the supermarket for ice cream.

With him gone, I wait for him to ring, as he sometimes did a dozen times a day.

With him gone, there is a place missing at the table and gaps in the fridge where bacon once sat.

With him gone, I'm trying to fill the space and it's not working.

Aidan was the reason our house had sound, the reason my children have better music knowledge than pretty much anyone else I know. The three of them shared noise, while I sat more happily in the quiet.

Aidan was the reason our house had mood. He refused overhead lighting. Bought second-hand lamps in op shops and fixed them up so he could control the colour and the light.

Aidan was the reason our house had style. I don't care about those things. The angle of the couch. The plump of the cushion. The green of the many indoor plants. Having lived for so many years on the things other people threw out, he could make a space from nothing. Find a rug in hard rubbish, repair an old table, sand back a butcher's block until it looked new. We used to joke that most of our furniture came from op shops or the side of the road. He never bought anything new. Instead, he scavenged for clothes, for records, for stories in the hand-me-downs of the world.

A few days after Aidan died, a light bulb blew in my cupboard, meaning I could barely make out which top to pull from the hanger. After that, I stopped bothering with changing my clothes, returning each day to the same slightly stale-smelling black cotton shirt that was as soft as the blanket my kids used as babies.

Then the fluorescent tube went in the kitchen, meaning I had to prepare food in semi-darkness. Then the fourth dining chair started leaking wood dust along the ground where the beam had snapped after someone had sat down too hard. Then the indoor plants started shrivelling and dropping leaves. Then my phone screen smashed. And then, the Bluetooth speaker stopped working and the stereo was silenced for the first day in many.

I took it as a series of grieving moments. That the inanimate objects that Aidan cared for decided they were on strike without him around.

So we lived in the dark. We sat on broken chairs. We avoided corners of our phones in case shards of glass worked their way into our thumbs. We played vinyl because we couldn't play anything else. We worked around him being gone.

And that was the saddest thing. Just getting on with it. I wanted to stop too. I was as broken as the chair. As chipped as my screen. As blown as the lightbulb.

Now I must learn how to do all these things without him. And what is hard is not the list of things you cannot do, but that you must suddenly learn them when you are at your worst.

One morning I woke feeling cheery and tackled Aidan's underwear drawer, until the sight of three coloured ratty handkerchiefs undid me and I sobbed into his mismatched pairs of socks. He always carried a hanky with him in his bag and would pull it out victoriously if one of the kids had a snotty nose, like somehow the hanky's very presence made him a better dad. I'd never considered his hankies before. But in that moment they were everything. I bundled up his socks, his underpants with the failing elastic, and his stretched bathers and shoved them into rubbish bags. Then I used each hanky to blow my nose and catch the tears.

I couldn't throw away anything else. The rest has been claimed by the kids. They slop around the house in his pilled oversized jumpers and his bleach-stained black t-shirts. I wear his pyjamas, preferring to remember them from before those final months when he had stopped wearing any because taking them down became too painful.

'It's all just stuff,' I can hear him say. He was a brutal minimalist. Each time he moved to a new house as a younger man, he would leave it all behind. We had a garage sale once in my parents' house after they moved. He sold an antique ventriloquist doll to a guy on a Harley-Davidson motorcycle for about twenty dollars. I can still see the bearded man riding off with the doll on his back, its head spinning around. The man couldn't believe the bargain he'd just been gifted. And Aidan seemed relieved to have one less thing to move.

Our daughter went hunting through old boxes. When I was in bed one night, she came to me with a love letter she'd found. It wasn't addressed to anyone and she wanted to know if it was intended for me or if Aidan had written it to someone else.

I couldn't remember him giving me the letter but, reading it, I knew it must have been mine. The sentiment of how he felt, of the things he said, was still very present. I also guessed that he probably wasn't storing love letters he'd written to other women in boxes destined for our garage.

I hope it cheered her thinking of her parents being so in love that letters were shared.

She found photographs too. Ones I'd never seen. Ones that captured the essence of Aidan from that other time, before sadness and age caught up with him. Ones of us when the worst thing we'd faced was waking up hungover. Photos of us delighting in each other.

I find myself trying to remember those times.

He had broad shoulders once. Arms tanned and strong. Hands that were often nicked with cuts from trying to fix something without the right tools. He had nuggety legs that could take him up a mountain. He'd told me once that he had short-twitch muscles which meant he was good on rugged terrain but not so great at long journeys. Short twitch always reminded me of a bird, and I imagined him inventing it to tease me.

★

Now when I remember him, I see images of him lying in a bed, one of the kids' ancient single doonas pulled tightly around him, his feet elevated and the cat curled somewhere close. Or it's of me helping him to the toilet, using our elaborate system of him standing, pivoting and landing on the seat of the hired walker, which I would then yank backwards, turn clumsily and try to wheel through the bedroom door towards the bathroom. Once when I'd tried this, early on, I'd drunk two negronis on a Zoom birthday call with my old friend and rammed him straight into the wall. Another night, I'd caught his feet under the wheel because he'd forgotten to tuck them up.

But the worst image that loops in my head sometimes when I wake in the middle of the night and look for his sleeping form next to me, is the time he fell. It was the last time we attempted using the walker. It was a Sunday night in late August. I'd helped him onto the toilet and left him to go because he still wanted that privacy, that rare control of his own body without witness. I returned when he called me, helped him to stand like we did, with his hands pushing down on the locked arms of the walker so that I could scoop up his pants and wait while he turned and sat back down on the small black plastic seat.

But this time, his arms shook and his legs wobbled. He started telling me to stop lifting the chair, which I couldn't understand because I was bracing it the same way I always had. Knowing something was wrong, I called for our daughter to help. She ran up from downstairs and held the walker while I tried to hold him, but he still thought we were lifting the walker up. I realised later it was because he was sinking but he couldn't fathom his body had failed so completely, and so the only thing that made sense was that we were raising the chair.

He crumpled onto himself, crying out in pain. His legs, which hurt to be touched, had concertinaed and he sank like the melting wicked witch in *The Wizard of Oz*. We helped him to lie flat on his back on the white tiled floor. He was crying. I sent our daughter out.

I tried to lift him up but couldn't. It was eight o'clock at night, during one of Melbourne's many Covid lockdowns, and I knew if I called an ambulance it could be hours before they arrived. It didn't feel like we had hours. So, I phoned a neighbour across the road. Told him I needed him.

Seconds later he appeared, as if magicked from some other time. Strong and muscled, he leant down and quietly explained what he was going to do. Confronted by a version of himself, Aidan stopped crying. This man was the same age, his children had gone to school with ours, he'd lived alongside us for years and he was about to heave Aidan up and save him from the indignity of lying on the bathroom floor.

Our neighbour positioned his hands under Aidan and gave me instructions on where to move the walker. Slowly, he lifted Aidan up and I wedged the walker in under him. This man helped me wheel Aidan back to bed and lifted him carefully, tenderly, back into position.

And then he told me, 'Anytime.' And he left.

I often think about how that affected our daughter, watching her once-strong father deflate on the floor. I tried to talk to her about it afterwards, but she told me it was fine. It was all fine.

Only it can't be.

Scene Five: Homeowner

The closest Aidan and I ever came to owning property together was with a series of second-hand tents. The first was a square mouldy canvas one we bought from a garage sale that smelt too bad to sleep in; the second was a lightweight four-person number borrowed from a friend that we never returned; and the third was a dome tent that had pegs missing and never quite looked like its photo when it was up.

    The houses we rented were similarly imperfect, but always home. When you're a renter, people often assume you aren't attached to the place you live in. As if by being a temporary guest you are somehow less sentimental, less house proud. Buying property on unceded land, we claim it as ours. We allocate such value to ownership in this country, believing it is only a mortgage that offers you the right to have a connection to place.

Act Three: Other Scenes

In 2020, when we left our peach-walled house in Charles Street that our friends owned, it was not by choice. We'd been there eight years, paying reduced rent because our friends were generous and kind. We'd raised our children in that house, grieved the loss of family, learnt about Aidan's cancer diagnosis, had parties, dinners and fights.

When my children talk about their memories of that house, they never mention the fact that it didn't belong to us. Instead, they fondly remember the front door mostly being open to anyone who dropped in, including the odd person who wandered in because the front door was open. They liked that they could always tell which parent was home by the noise levels. If it was Aidan, music would be blaring; if it was me, the house would be quiet.

We had to move quickly from that house because it was being sold and, because of Aidan's cancer, we didn't want to move far. We took a lease on the only affordable place I could find within walking distance. It was a three-storey newish townhouse on an intersecting street. The fact that we took it despite it having so many stairs suggests we had no idea that Aidan would soon be bedbound, confined to his room long before he needed to be because he couldn't manage them. The townhouse was ugly, but Aidan made of it what he could, buying a second-hand couch for the kids, and setting up the garage as a music room and space for their friends. From the balcony we could see the old place, the apple trees being ripped out and replaced with something ornamental and neat. The native garden being binned to make way for the perfect lawn.

I kept watch for our rubber plant. The one we bought as a pair at a garage sale in St Kilda when we first started living together.

The seller was Russian and he told us a tale in his thick accent about the rubber plants who were lovers and who should not be separated. In fresh love ourselves, we bought the story and the plants, and carried them home in our arms. Only one survived. Outgrowing pots and spots in the house, we moved it many times, until it settled in a large plastic-bottomed tub in the garden in Charles Street. The roots cracked the plastic and escaped into the ground and when it came time to move it, we found we couldn't. We had to leave it behind. A symbol of us in that house.

I kept waiting to see it in the skip, thinking that I'd pull it out and rescue it. But it must be still there. Burrowing deeper and deeper into the soil so that nobody will ever make it leave.

When Aidan died, my son's primary school teachers sent me a rubber plant with dark green leaves. They didn't know the story of the original one that we'd left behind.

Now, the new one is in a cream pot in my new apartment. It's not part of a romantic pair. It is a one. Like me.

Aidan used to spend hours driving around and around doing recces of houses he'd found on the internet. Places 'we might', 'we may', 'we could' buy if everything aligned. I resented those trips and his attempts to take me. I'd point out something wrong with the place, poke a hole in his dream, tear it down with doubts and well-placed criticism: 'It's too far for the kids to get to school.' 'It's on a main road and is too noisy.' 'It's dark and poky and probably has asbestos in the walls. And the ceiling.'

Act Three: Other Scenes

And so it went.

We did try to buy, though. Many times we almost had enough money for a deposit, then one of us was out of work for a while and we'd spend our savings. We were outbid at auctions. We even made an offer once for a house we were renting – a run-down place with an outside bathroom and gaps under the doors. The landlord responded to the offer by putting up our rent.

The truth? I didn't think buying property would work out for us, so I shut it down before it could. Instead, I pretended, loudly, obnoxiously, that I was fine with renting. Fine with a capital 'F'. And I mostly was. Back then.

Until Aidan died at home in a rented bedroom on the second floor and I became scared. Scared of having to find rent that I couldn't pay. Scared of being made to move every year. Scared of arguing with the real estate agent for basic repairs.

And scared of being untethered to a physical place because I was already so unmoored emotionally.

Some people believe that giving you advice about buying property is helpful. As if you've been waiting all these years for them to tell you: 'It's time. Do it soon or it will be too late.' As if, somehow, you are unaware of being left behind.

In the final year before Aidan died, we stopped looking at houses. Stopped pretending it was ever going to happen. He wanted me to reassure him that I'd buy a place after he died. Use the money from his death benefits for something useful. I promised him I would.

The market was flat when he died. Fourteen months of

lockdowns in Melbourne had finally managed to put a dint in the ever-increasing property market. People said it was 'the perfect time to buy'.

But after Aidan died, I wasn't up to buying anything, except chocolate and gin. I ignored the market, banked the death benefits and continued to pay all my monthly earnings to live in the concrete trap of a townhouse with patches of mould and ugly brown biscuit-shaped bricks. I couldn't afford the rent. Not as a single mother on an irregular writer's income. And each month I would dread having to find all those dollars.

Following in his father's footsteps, our son had taken up the real estate hunt. And one night he found a place. A long, thin, converted shopfront on a main road. It was, according to the ad: *Retro and unique. Charming and bright.* My son wanted us to 'take a look'. He was tired of the endless promises about one day having his own room, about one day painting walls and knocking in nails to hang paintings wherever we chose.

So, we looked. Him and me. And the house was quirky. And the house would work. And I felt draped in sadness as he raced through room by room, just like his dad would have, looking for potential, looking for where things might go.

I found a bank and told some lies. Was offered a mortgage.

We took another look at the house. This time dragging my daughter along. I chatted the whole way there. She was quiet, judging how far away it was from her friends, her school, her streets. But when we stepped inside, she liked it too. And when we spied a copy of one of my books on display in the child's bedroom, we took it as a sign. The house could be ours.

The auction was Friday.

Act Three: Other Scenes

That Friday afternoon, my daughter came home from school with two friends. We talked about the house and how I had all my ducks lined up, how I could bid and how we could be moving in thirty days if the settlement was short.

One of my daughter's friends said it was miles away. The other said they couldn't walk to school together if we moved. It wasn't miles away, but it was enough. Outside the small radius we'd lived in since our children were born. Away from the incidental meetings in the street where we knew our community.

It was enough to get me thinking as I carried a pile of books across the road to one of our old neighbours on Charles Street. They'd built their house while we still lived next door. It was large and lovely, full of herbs and happy places to sit. I remembered the site from before they owned it, when it was home to a tatty blue weatherboard. One afternoon, a friend had climbed up a ladder at our place and looked across and seen a bag of marijuana hiding in the gutter of the weatherboard and he'd left it there for the rain.

The books were a stack of my daughter's treasures from when she was younger and I handed them over for my neighbour's children. We talked about herbs and she told me to push the gate open whenever I liked and pick what I needed. As I left her front yard that day and walked down the street that I'd walked so many times with Aidan, I cried.

He was there in the front yard of our old house, pulling up weeds. He was there with an umbrella, running a lemonade stall with our son. He was there holding my hand as we walked to a restaurant on date night.

For twenty-two years I'd lived with him on these streets and little had changed. Some of the old Greek and Italian families had sold up and moved away. But their houses still mostly stood.

That night when I was supposed to be bidding for the renovated shopfront on Zoom, I made an excuse. Said the finance had fallen through. Told my daughter we would stay on our streets, rent forever if we had to.

But you can't always rent forever in the streets you love because it is no longer the affordable, run-down suburb you moved to all those years ago. It is full of aspiration and renovation. Renters are at the whim of one-year leases and landlords who drag their heels with repairs and rent increases. We're being priced out of the suburbs where our children have gone to school, where the streets are familiar, where we feel connected.

It was cheaper for me to pay a mortgage than to pay rent. But banks don't like lending money to those of us with insecure income and irregular tax returns.

Several months later, our real estate agent rang to tell me the owners of the ugly townhouse were selling and we'd have to move. None of us liked the townhouse, but finding affordable rental properties was nearly impossible.

My son ramped up his home ownership search, needing perhaps to be in control of something in this out-of-control time. He told me about the apartment for sale at the end of the street. I'd been intrigued by the block for years. It had been built in the 1920s, originally as a factory for underpants and socks, and it seemed solid and dependable.

We went to the open for inspection. The apartment was big and light, and the small first-floor balcony looked onto the slate

Act Three: Other Scenes

steeple of the church where Aidan and I used to op-shop together on a Saturday.

I couldn't afford it.

My son was stoic when I told him, brushing it off like he didn't care, but we both knew we had a couple of months to find a new place to live and neither of us wanted to leave the area.

When the apartment was passed in at auction, a spiritual friend called it a 'sign'. I wasn't convinced that it was anything more than a crack of good luck. But I still couldn't afford it.

Then a generous friend offered to lend me the shortfall. I squeezed a bit extra out of the mortgage broker and put in an offer that was accepted in November 2021 with a thirty-day settlement.

We had to start packing.

I rang friends to tell them and felt touched by their efforts at enthusiasm, sensing they understood why I was so reluctant to celebrate. I knew I *should* be happy. At the age of fifty, I was a statistical anomaly. Most of us will never own property if we haven't bought by then.

The truth was that it had taken my partner dying for me to do this. And even still, the death benefits weren't quite enough for a deposit. It had taken a village for me to buy a place of my own. Dad helped a bit, my friend lent a bit and the bank lent a lot. I was lucky to have people around me who could step in when I needed them. Luckier than many in this, 'the lucky country'.

Friends arrived to help us move, wrapping glasses, boxing books, driving carloads down the road to the new place. One afternoon, we shifted the many bottles of wine, gin and whiskey that had been sent after Aidan died. A stranger laughed at the gentle clinking of the glass, joking that he'd be around later, as we rolled the trolley along the concrete to the door of the apartment.

Half in, half out, we weren't officially living anywhere as we took weeks to move things by hand, trying to reduce the load the removalists would shift, because it was cheaper that way.

Five days before the van was due to arrive and collect all the big stuff, Melbourne was hit by a raging storm. Water rose fast, blocking drains and kissing the bottom of cars. Our street flooded as we stayed inside, boxing up our belongings.

My daughter was away for the storm, staying with a friend for a couple of nights. We'd planned that her room would be the last to move because she was in the cupboard-sized space on the bottom floor of the townhouse and it would be easy to shift her things.

When she returned home on Friday night and opened her bedroom door, she screamed. I ran down the stairs, without any understanding of what I'd find.

The skylight overhead had leaked during the storm and everything was soaked. The carpet was still spongy, the air smelt dank and damp, and mould was already flowering in patches.

She snatched up a pile of Aidan's records from the floor. The covers were damp and had started to buckle. I didn't want her removing everything before the real estate agent had been to assess the damage, so I stopped her taking anything else out.

When he arrived, he was barely sympathetic and told me to call my insurance company.

It turned ugly between the owners and the real estate and me. They doubled down and started questioning whose fault it was and I struggled to argue, even knowing they were the guilty party.

My daughter lost everything: the space-age sound system that Aidan had bought for her thirteenth birthday, my mum's old sewing machine that she'd inherited, books, clothes, photographs, letters and all her stuff. Irreplaceable.

Even now she sometimes pulls on a dress that has been through the wash to find a mould stain that refuses to leave.

I don't think I dealt with the room flooding with the sort of sympathy she needed. I was barely afloat in those weeks, packing up our lives, moving house and leaving behind the room where Aidan had died. I was off kilter, incapable of just holding her and understanding what she'd lost.

It was a sort of fog that wouldn't lift. The mortgage was cheaper than my rent and I could paint the walls any colour I liked. But Aidan wasn't with me. He wasn't there laughing at the Monopoly set the real estate agent insisted I take when they handed me the keys, helping me pull up the ugly rug that the old owners had left behind, arguing with me about where to hang our art.

That first night we slept on mattresses on the floor of the new apartment. My son didn't have a bedroom because we were building walls to create one for him, so he was in the lounge for a couple of months. My daughter didn't have a bed because she'd lost hers in the flood, so she was on a borrowed mattress until the insurance money came through.

And for the first time in twenty-five years, I had a bedroom without Aidan.

Scene Six: Hypochondria

The Greek origins of the word hypochondria can be broken into two: *hypo* and *chondria*. *Hypo* means underneath and *chondria* means cartilage. Together, they mean the soft organs beneath your ribs and sternum. The reason the meaning fascinates me is because I have often visited my doctor with a generalised pain in this area. A pain that seems to have no fixed address.

I know my health anxiety stems from stress or grief or fear. It flares up when someone I love dies and it can take months to settle.

The first time I became a hypochondriac, I was thirty-three and a dear friend had died from melanoma. I can still recall the conversation we had at a dinner party when she told a bunch of us that she'd found a suspicious mole, but it would all be okay. I had a newborn baby, and I wasn't sleeping. Fearful that my moles were changing too, I started seeing a dermatologist and never quite believed her when she examined my skin,

Act Three: Other Scenes

declared it okay and sent me on my way.

The second time, I was forty-two and Mum had just died. Watching my mother's determination to breathe while her lungs drowned in pleural effusions, I'd struggled with overwhelming guilt. Unlike her, I'd smoked when I was younger. The more I thought about my own lungs in relation to my mother's, the guiltier I felt. And the guiltier I felt, the more convinced I became that I too would develop lung cancer.

I booked an appointment with the doctor I'd been seeing for many years and told her I was short of breath. She tested my oxygen levels with an oximetry. It was ninety-eight per cent. Then she did a lung function test called a spirometry. Connected to a machine, I breathed into a mouthpiece like I was being tested for my blood alcohol levels by police on the side of the road. This told my doctor about lung capacity and airflow. The results revealed 'nothing sinister' and were 'very normal', but I was unmoved. Her attempts to reassure me fell short.

Then she began asking questions about my stress levels. I told her about my mother dying. She nodded, typed into her computer like this was getting to the nub of the matter. We talked about grief and guilt. Her voice measured, she suggested a therapist, explaining that shortness of breath is one of the most common medical symptoms. She also told me it's far more common for it to mean anxiety or stress than something more serious.

I didn't believe her. I decided she'd missed something critical. At my insistence, she sent me for an X-ray. I stood in front of the machine in a thin medical gown and had my chest X-rayed, convinced they'd find a tumour to rival my mother's.

They found nothing.

After Aidan died, my hypochondria flared up again. In the months after his death, I was convinced I had a melanoma (I didn't), bowel cancer (I didn't) and, most recently, a brain tumour.

The tumour fear began when the tinnitus that I'd had for some time worsened in my left ear. After ignoring it for a few weeks, I made an appointment to see my doctor. When I arrived at the clinic, I was flustered, running late. It was hot, one of those unusual early autumn days that hit the mid-thirties. By the time I was buzzed inside, I was sweaty and when I lowered my head to the machine that checked the temperature of every patient, the nurse told me that it read thirty-seven point eight degrees and I needed to follow her to the fever clinic.

I tried to explain but sounded like I was somehow justifying an illness. I sat and waited in the small room until my doctor came in. She checked my head. I was back to thirty-six point five degrees. She apologised for making me wait, said a lot of people were coming in for a cry now because they hadn't seen anyone for so long due to Covid. Then she asked me if I needed a cry too. I probably did, but not there.

I told her about my ear. She looked inside with a torch and we talked about tinnitus and the fact it was worse in my left. She suggested a hearing test and a visit to an ENT specialist. She knows how I feel about medical procedures and understands where my brain goes when something goes wrong with my body. She even rang me when Aidan died to see if I was okay.

I left with a referral and a worry.

On the day of the hearing test, I was plugged into a machine and a student watched on, learning. The audiologist explained what would happen. I had to press a button whenever I heard a sound.

Act Three: Other Scenes

I pressed, over and over, thinking how well I was doing, pleased with myself.

When they finished, the audiologist explained my hearing was down. But it was both ears. Not just my left. I needed another test. One to check if my brain was registering sound or if there was a problem with the nerves.

I left convinced there was something wrong.

Aidan had a sore back. He bought a six-class pass to Pilates that did nothing because it was cancer breaking free of his prostate and snaking its way through his body.

I googled. Diagnosed myself with an acoustic neuroma, a benign tumour that could be deadly because of where it grows.

The following test said my nerves were fine. But now I needed to see the ENT about the tinnitus and work out why my hearing was diminished. The specialist I was sent to asked if I worked with jackhammers. I told him I was a writer and he joked about the noise of a quill on the page. He showed me where my hearing should have been sitting and where it does, like I'd spent my life around explosions or heavy equipment. I told him I spent my twenties standing in front of very loud speakers at pubs watching live bands.

He thought that might have caused it, but he didn't really know. He told me he was sending me off for an MRI because it would be negligent not to. I must have pulled a face because he tried to be reassuring and tell me it was probably nothing. He didn't think I had a tumour.

Still, I left with a piece of paper that said they needed to scan my brain to make sure.

The more I worried, the more my ears rang and pulsed.

★

When I pulled up in the car park behind the medical practice in Richmond for my MRI at seven in the morning, I realised it was where I brought Aidan for a PET scan all those months ago to assess how far the cancer had spread. Because of Covid, I had to leave him in his gown and wander Bridge Road until he phoned, and we drove home quietly, talkback radio filling the gaps where our chatter used to be.

I was trying not to see the coincidence as a sign.

The woman who took me through made me swap my mask for one without metal across the nose because of the MRI machine. I lay down and tried to relax as I was reversed inside the barrel. I think I cried, imagining my kids without both of us, imagining the mess in my head.

Afterwards, I dressed and left and drove home through the city.

I thought about the strange 'after' of an appointment: leaving a hospital, walking out of a waiting room, sitting with the knowledge you didn't have minutes earlier. I thought about how many times Aidan and I heard news, our hands letting go as the doctor walked in. How many times had we hoped? How many takeaway coffees had we bought? And doughnuts had we shared? And hours had we waited to see someone who would fill in another small block of information?

I decided not to think about my brain or my ears or anything else.

Instead, I saw my dentist, who thought that perhaps I was grinding my teeth, clenching my jaw so tight on the left that my hearing was maybe affected. She asked, 'Are you stressed?'

And I laughed.

It's all I am.

★

Act Three: Other Scenes

Speaking with friends, it seems many of them have become fixated on the idea of their own mortality while caring for a dying parent. After their parent goes, they start to hunt backwards for evidence of who they were now that their holder of childhood stories has left. I know Mum's death is where my obsession with remembering my past started.

But my hypochondria was different after Aidan's death. It was not only born of a fear of me dying; it was also about our children and my fear that if I go too then they would have no-one steering them through.

A friend who'd recovered from breast cancer told me that when her youngest child turned eighteen, she finally stopped fearing dying and leaving her children without a mother because, if the worst happened, at least they were adults.

After Aidan died, I suspect the kids worried about me dying as well. It's not only my fear, but theirs too. The books they read as children played out the narrative of the orphan, the lost, the parentless. I hear stories of people who won't travel in the same plane as their partner in case it crashes and kills them both.

I realised I am the age that Aidan was when he died.

The specialist called. My brain was fine. He told me to stop working with jackhammers because I'd probably need a hearing aid one day. I resisted asking when.

Scene Seven:
Stuff

The relationship that humans have with stuff is changing. Once our houses groaned with collections of books, records, letters, postcards and photographs. Now much of this can be stored digitally, not even on a device, but in a cloud somewhere. But perhaps this new-found reliance on technology is undone when someone dies. Then the currency of memory plays its part and we become desperate to hold on to things that have become synonymous with a time and with a person.

My son jokes with me that I'm giving away his childhood when I suggest handing on a pair of hot-pink Dr. Martens that he wore at four. He is only partly joking, but I understand his grappling with giving things up since his dad died.

In the pile of stuff that I rescued when my parents sold my childhood home was a shell-crusted jewellery box. It was a present from a dear friend of my dad's that I immediately treasured because

Act Three: Other Scenes

I treasured her. It was circular and blue and made from an empty Nivea face-cream pot. Mum used Nivea and I considered it to be the height of sophistication. I sometimes watched from the bathroom doorway as she smeared the thick white cream on her face and neck, and if I was lucky, she'd dot some across my cheeks.

As a child, I believed that Dad's friend had crafted the jewellery box with me in mind. She'd stuck shells all over the Nivea pot so that only snatches of the identifying bright blue plastic could be seen. Believing it to be homemade raised its value, because it meant her attachment to me was so great that she would scour the beaches for the finest shells and spend hours constructing a puzzle of them, gluing each one into the right place to create the desired effect.

Now I know that it's unlikely it was made by her. She probably just found it at a market somewhere and picked it up because it was sweet. But whenever I think about it, I still like to pretend.

I never stored jewellery in that box. Except for treasuring a butterfly ring from a vending machine and a couple of Hello Kitty hair clips, my most important collection was dead spiders. I particularly loved the huntsman spiders that lived inside our house, their bodies angular and arthritic-looking after they were dead, and the trapdoor spiders that made their homes between the bricks in the backyard and could only be found with patience and luck. Huntsman spiders outnumbered the rarer spiders in the box, and I was always on the lookout for a redback. They would often nest underneath the plastic swing that hung unused in our front garden. I never found a dead one. Only live ones.

The dead spiders went into my jewellery box, squashed on top of each other, and over time they would drop limbs and crumble into a pile of brown dust. I was always careful not to move the box too rapidly in case it sped up the disintegration process.

I still have that spider collection. And cuttings from my eight-year-old ponytail, a stuffed toy I slept with at six, and picture books that shaped my earliest years. Since Mum died, I have held on to clothes I will never wear and books I remember her liking, simply because they mean connection to a time with her.

When Aidan was working as a cleaner, a friend employed him to help sort out a property before it was sold. They were told the house belonged to a hoarder. A professional woman in her sixties who owned a large and impressive mid-century property. One room at the front had been maintained for entertaining, but the rest of the ten rooms were bursting with stuff. The bathroom was decorated wall to ceiling with empty boxes of cask wine and the toilet was almost covered by layers and layers of newspapers that had been levelled to the same height as the seat.

They filled seven skips with rubbish from the house. Bags full of ingredients for complete meals that had been bought and left on the kitchen bench, rotting where they stayed. Cartons of unopened milk that had hardened. Enough toothpaste for an entire school of students. Cupboards of clothes never worn.

There was even a car, which they discovered in the garage. It was hidden, like it had been parked there years ago and forgotten. It was a twelve-cylinder Morgan, handmade in England in the seventies. The keys had been left in the ignition and when Aidan's friend turned them, the engine started on the very first try.

Act Three: Other Scenes

Compulsive hoarding is a clinical disorder but is often bandied about cruelly as a joke. When Aidan met the woman who lived in the house, he was stunned by her manner. She didn't acknowledge her living environment; she talked to him about literature. She looked manicured and he couldn't work out how she could maintain any sort of self-care because her shower was cut off from use by boxes. He later found out that she had her hair styled once a week in a salon and bought new clothes whenever she needed to change outfits.

When my grandmother died, my father and his siblings found thousands of dollars of new clothes that she'd bought but had never worn. My grandmother wasn't a hoarder, but she did hold on to things. Just like other members of my family. Me too perhaps. Like my safety net of books that I stack near my bed just in case I'm trapped inside with nothing to do.

I have never wanted to live in a museum resembling my past, but each change to my surroundings causes another break with Aidan. The apartment is divided into the purchase of objects he was present for and those he was not. Instead of buying new chairs or rugs or sculptures that he hasn't seen, I allow myself to retrieve things from my childhood because even if he didn't know them, they still existed at the same time as he did.

Our apartment is sparsely furnished because of this. There is space in the loungeroom and the dining room because what I owned with Aidan doesn't fill it. So, instead of buying me presents now, my dad is gifting me things from the past. Things he knows I love. Recently it was a chair that I'd grown up sitting in.

A chair born around the same time as me, which Dad spent all his wages (and company discount) on when he was just an apprentice copywriter working at Myer in the late 1960s.

The story goes that the chair was a one-off in Australia, a display model that Myer had imported from Brazil, hoping to sell many. But it was too expensive for the time and for the market, and so the chair that my dad bought is the only one to ever make it here.

Aidan would have sat in the chair at some point in our visits to my family, and so it is not a hefty change introducing it into our place. It is a long slouchy tan leather armchair with a foot stool. The frame is metal and the legs are heavy wooden blocks of dark brown mahogany. There's tan rope webbing holding it all together and it has aged far better than I have.

Until it arrived at my house, the chair was one of many in Dad's loungeroom, rarely sat on since we left home. I like to think that it was just waiting to be useful again.

It is one of those chairs that once you're in, you forget any reason you might have to leave it. And at one time or another, we all succumbed to its comfort. Often it was a place to rest after a big night or somewhere to sleep off a hangover.

It was even blamed for ruining Christmas lunch sometime in the mid-eighties. Mum wasn't much of a drinker, but she had a yearly tradition with her friend to drink Brandy Alexanders for breakfast. Shaking together the brandy, crème de cacao and cream in the silver aluminium cocktail shaker when her friend dropped in with a plate of homemade crisp Crostoli biscuits dusted in icing sugar, Mum danced around the kitchen. Usually, they stopped at one and returned to their own houses to prepare Christmas lunch, but that year, they kept drinking.

Act Three: Other Scenes

By ten am, Mum was giggling and by eleven she was asleep, in the chair, in the middle of the loungeroom. And for three hours she slept. We crept around her, only waking her up when the extended family arrived expecting a meal. The turkey had never made it to the oven, so we had Vegemite sandwiches for lunch. I wonder now why one of us didn't just turn the oven on to cook the turkey. Perhaps we were so charmed by the sight of Mum napping that we lost all ability to be helpful, although it's more likely we were just too lazy.

But that is the reputed power of the chair.

I move the chair into our small loungeroom, near the bookshelves. My son tells me it should be in the corner, facing out. We often disagree about the arrangement of furniture. And it is not uncommon for him to move things he thinks look better somewhere else. It is one of the many traits he has inherited from his dad. There were times when I would come home from work and Aidan would have rearranged the entire house.

While I'm down the street buying ingredients for dinner, the chair is moved and, as much as I rant about the house being mine, I leave it in the new position because my son is right – it looks much better.

Next to the chair, he places a wobbly tiled coffee table I rescued from hard rubbish. The wood is buckled in places where it was sitting too long in the rain, so it isn't as sturdy as it should be, but it does the job of displaying a mid-century brutalist sculpture my dad recently let me take from his house. The sculpture is another piece of furniture that looms large in my childhood, made by one of Dad's friends in the seventies. Epitomising the time, it is a blend of dark wood and large abstract shapes in heavy silver metal. As kids, we would allocate meaning to the shapes, believing it to be a whale with its broad tail flipped up in the air. The whale-tail piece slips out of the larger fixed block and you can hold it in your hands, the metal cold and smooth to touch.

My memory of the sculpture was that it felt alive, as if it was part of the family, never staying too long in one room, but moving around the house at will.

When I tell my brother about the sculpture coming to live with me, he tells me he wants it too. And I fight the guilt that I've relocated something we both love, telling him I only have it on loan.

The cat has decided that she doesn't like me sitting on the chair because, like all new things that arrive in our house, it is hers. It is hers until she decides it is not. She leaps up and digs in a claw until I move one leg and then the other, and then she settles on the foot stool, circling herself until she stops, and promptly goes to sleep, leaving my feet with nowhere to go.

When I lie in the chair, my head resting on the softest goat leather, I venture back. Back to the time of the red-and-black patterned seventies rug that covered our hard slate floors, where I learnt to crawl and walk and talk and read. Back to a time when dinner would be corned beef and braised cabbage, or casserole that my brother would call 'wet meat'. Back to the time when I shared my bed with twenty teddies and stuffed horses and elephants, and most of them would last the night curled against me.

This home is long gone, sold off many years ago, but perhaps I am trying to recreate corners. Maybe in my attempt at rescuing

Act Three: Other Scenes

furniture from before, I am trying to bridge the who I was as a child with the who I am now.

I saved the red-and-black rug that Dad was tossing out and brought it home. Threads are pulled and the colour is faded in patches but still it feels the same under my bare feet as it did when I was a kid.

The cat uses it as a toy, each night galloping from the other end of the room and jumping on, riding the rug along the polished floorboards to where she crashes into the back door. Each morning I straighten the rug out and return it to its spot, and each night the cat climbs on and slides.

There are other things I covet in Dad's house: the painting of a woman's face with brown bobbed hair that I've always seen as Mum, a heavy black metal frypan my parents bought many years ago that cooked the meals of my youth, and the brown Arabia ware dinner plates that we ate off every night.

But Dad is as sentimental as I am. He won't part with most of it.

I fear that I am attempting time travel with the liberation of these things. It began with Mum's death when I started looking backwards for her. And now that Aidan's gone too, I'm doing that in double speed. It's not just because I'm trying to find them both again. It's also because I'm trying to return to a version of myself that is a long way from death.

There was safety in childhood. Death was not yet coming for me.

Most things in our house have belonged to someone else. Heirlooms, hand-me-downs, op-shop finds and treasures rescued from hard rubbish. I've bought so little I don't even know what I like. The fact that almost everything we owned is second-hand is not only due to having limited money; Aidan hated shopping in actual shops. He liked the hunt, the possibility that each time he entered an op shop he might find a unicorn. And he often did.

The thrill of gambling on entering a shop to find something rare is a little like writing a play that may or may not be produced. Everything has potential to change your life, but there is no certainty in any of it.

Our dining table once belonged to Aidan's parents. It's a hulking lump of wood with carved legs, rounded at either end. There's a split down the middle of the tabletop where Aidan poked peas as a child. I've started hunting out vintage tablecloths to cover it up because I've never liked it. Neither did he. But we could never justify buying a new one.

And now our son is attached to it. It is the table of his childhood and he won't consider me replacing it with something more elegant. He likes that he has played cards here and learnt to use chopsticks. That he has eaten at it with friends – new and old. That the table has moved from house to house to house to house, and that the cat sits at it with us in the evenings when we dine. My son stuck a plaque on the back of one of the chairs that says *Aiden Fennessy*. A theatre company made it and misspelt his name. We found it funny and endearing because it happened so often in his professional career. And now that chair is forever Aidan's.

I'm stuck with this table for as long as our son remains attached.

He has let me toss other things, though: broken lamps, an ugly bookshelf, one of Aidan's hats. But he has kept the watches and the jumpers, the glasses and the coats. The other day, I found him teaching himself guitar on Aidan's untuned acoustic that has never sounded great.

I'm undecided about whether I'm becoming less attached to stuff or more. When I discover that I've left a sunhat Aidan bought me on an Auckland bus, I phone the lost property office, but the number rings out. Flying home, I remember that Aidan didn't even like it much when he gave it to me.

Things hold such importance after death. And reducing someone to their life's possessions immediately increases the value of each one. It is why we fight with siblings over things we don't even want when parents die. As if we can better understand the person we've lost if only we can crack the code to the object's importance in their lives. And this need for closeness stops us from throwing things out.

Because Aidan cared so little for stuff, it is not his childhood table that I require, but scribbled notes inside books, letters written to others, a shopping list, a reminder to change a scene in an unfinished play. He was made of words: sharp-witted and funny. And it is in words that I can find him.

Scene Eight:
Isolation

When Aidan was dying, I washed the shopping in the sink to keep germs out of our house. The doctors had been clear about what Covid could do to someone in the final stages of cancer. None of us wanted to be responsible for it entering our lives.

When Covid did arrive eighteen months after Aidan had died, it was the Thursday before the Easter holidays and we had plans. We were eating breakfast, ready to go rollerskating, when my son said he should do a test first because he'd been vomiting and had felt faint the night before.

As I shovelled in my baked beans on toast, he stuck the swiper up his nose. One minute later he said, 'Oh no.' I thought he was joking because we did that a lot. Once he'd even drawn a second red line onto his test and tried to trick me.

We both stared at the two lines. They were equally bright. No mistake. I gave him another RAT, a different brand, just in case. That was positive too. The three of us were now back inside for seven days.

He went to his room and I went to collect his sister from her job in a bookshop. I made phone calls from the car, warning friends we'd seen the day before.

Dreading my daughter's reaction as her school holidays disappeared, I was surprised when she seemed relieved at the thought of seven days inside with nothing to do but lie in bed and watch television.

I was immediately edgy. My head ached, my throat too and I knew I must be positive. I did my own test. Nothing. And another. Still nothing.

A friend told me she'd been the same when her daughter tested positive, but she didn't. She told me it was probably all in my head.

By Easter Saturday, my daughter and I were still negative. I lay in my bed writing while she pottered around her room. I could hear the water running and the shampoo bottle hit the ground.

My son called out from time to time for a snack or a drink. Sometimes he appeared with an N95 mask on and I followed him back into his room with a spray can of eucalyptus.

He spent his days researching a new drum kit. He already had one. A seventies model I added to after his dad died. He jokes sometimes about all the money I spent on him that month. How I was grotesquely generous, as if by spending up big I'd erase all that my children had experienced over the past year as they'd watched their dad die.

I wasn't buying this second kit. He was. It was expensive too. So, he'd been selling off things from his room, from his collection. He's always been a bit of a collector like his uncle and his grandfather. It runs in my family.

As if proving to me that he could be ruthless, he started texting me photos of all the things he was prepared to sell, with prices for them. I wasn't sure that he'd manage to find a buyer to spend one hundred dollars on a tin car he'd pulled from a skip five years ago, but he assured me it was a Japanese original from the 1960s. And sure enough, he was right. I told him I thought he had a job flipping retro objects, just like his uncle did. He grinned at me through the glass in his bedroom door, his mask on his chin.

When we built my son's room after we'd moved in, he'd picked the door he wanted: an old rustic thing that our builder had found on the side of the road, it was panelled with squares of glass and had wood that was lacquered in years of paint. When it was installed, the builder half stripped it, so the wood was wood again and the glass was clean and without smudges. Now there were fingerprints dancing on either side, as my son and I pressed our hands to the glass, pretending we could touch without sharing germs.

My son was talking to me through the glass of his bedroom door again about the drum kit he'd found. I explained he couldn't buy it until he was out of isolation and we could go and have a look at it. He held up his laptop so I could see the brown-veneered drums, the set-up.

He's been a drummer since he was six. My parents bought him his first single drum for Christmas and he's played ever since.

Act Three: Other Scenes

Since we moved to the apartment, he hadn't been able to drum. He was waiting for me to have some spare cash so I could pay to have the small spare room soundproofed. Because he couldn't drum, he was teaching himself Gary Numan songs on a little eighties Casio keyboard he'd bought from a man at the junk market we go to.

But for the past few days, he'd been silent. Covid had knocked him around, affected his hearing. He hadn't played the bass guitar or the keyboard or any of the large stack of vinyl that he'd bought himself. He'd been the quietest I'd ever known him to be.

He wasn't even hungry. My teenage boy who can demolish a loaf of bread in a day had barely eaten in three.

As days continued to pass without us getting Covid, my daughter and I spent hours thinking about meals. The next one. The one after. It was how we split up time. Coffee in the mornings. Toast to break our fast. Lunch was long and messy and I wiped down the benches after she'd cooked. By dinnertime I wasn't even hungry, but I ate anyway.

Over the 2020 lockdowns in Melbourne, when Aidan was at his worst and I couldn't leave the house, friends delivered treats. After he died, our house was once again groaning with food.

Thanks to my son's Covid, we were back in isolation. The sunshine was strong outside and it was Easter – a long weekend of family and friends. We should have been seeing people. But we weren't. Instead, our friends texted: *Do you want anything? Do you need anything? Can we drop off anything?*

My daughter's friends were the first: blueberry muffins, still warm. Then bars of chocolate and flowers picked from a beach holiday followed. My brother came with gelati in a tub and cones wrapped in brown paper to stop them cracking. A friend delivered bread and fruit and vitamins. Another dropped a bag of shopping from the market. I buzzed each of them into the building and then waited to hear them leave. Then I masked up and snuck outside to retrieve the treats from the doormat.

We felt loved. We felt remembered. Just like we did when Aidan was dying. But it took me back too. To those days when I couldn't leave, when I was trapped with him in the house, waiting to be needed.

It took me back to those months where I felt dangerously lost.

Others have said that isolation with Covid has returned them to the trauma of the two years of lockdowns and restrictions during the pandemic. And I understand why. I thought seven days would be a breeze. I'd do some work, pull out a jigsaw puzzle, make bread like I never really got around to the first time.

Instead, I tried not to think about Aidan in that room in the old house.

Lockdowns cut us off. Trapped us away like Rapunzel in her castle. And it was happening again.

On day four I found a hair elastic in the cat's poo.

She was the only one enjoying us being home.

My son still had his door shut and the cat pawed at the glass, trying to get in.

My daughter and I ended up taking advantage of her brother isolating in his room, watching films he had no interest in.

Act Three: Other Scenes

The first night was *Official Secrets* starring Keira Knightley as a low-level spy who leaks an email to the press to try to stop England from going to war with Iraq. It was a compromise because I wanted a spy film and my daughter wanted a newspaper scandal.

The following night we continued the newspaper theme with Oscar-winning *Spotlight*. I'd seen it before, but like most films I've watched, I'd forgotten half of the story. We were both happy watching Mark Ruffalo play a character who doesn't turn green. *Spotlight* is loosely based on a series of stories run by the *Boston Globe*'s specialist investigative team who uncovered the Catholic Church-sanctioned movement of paedophile priests in Boston after claims of abuse surfaced.

Aidan was raised Catholic and he tackled the church and its cover-up of systemic abuse in the last play he wrote. My own parents were not raised with religion. As a young adult my mum decided she wanted to know about religion and became a Sunday School teacher for about nine months. She ditched it after she married and was a devout disbeliever until she was diagnosed with cancer and started a journey as a Buddhist. She used to say she wanted something to help her with death and the hours she spent meditating seemed to do that.

Aidan had long ago left the church, but in the week before he died when his sleep was heavy and strained, I woke one night to him chanting, 'Our Father, Who art in Heaven, Hallowed be Thy Name; Thy Kingdom come; Thy Will be done, On Earth as it is in Heaven.'

I tried to wake him, but his eyes were shut tight and the words were coming from deep within. Our son woke up too, unnerved.

I ushered him back to bed and tried to lighten the moment, but it was clear he was as shaken as I was. It was three in the morning and it was like Aidan was in a trance.

I phoned the night nurse at the palliative care ward. She told me to use the blue drops. They were for agitation.

'Is he agitated?' she asked.

I laughed, uncomfortably. 'I'm not sure, but I am. I can't wake him.'

I took the small vial of medicine and dropped three spots of blue inside his crusted lips. Within minutes, the chanting had stopped and he'd settled.

I lay awake on the floor beside him, wanting to tell him what had just happened. The old Aidan would have been intrigued, but even in the morning when he was lucid and awake, this Aidan didn't really understand.

Another night in iso, and it was my turn to choose a film. I picked Ben Stiller's directorial debut, *Reality Bites*, released in 1994. I had strong memories of it, having seen it many times at the cinema I once worked in. It's a romantic comedy about a bunch of newly graduated twenty-something-year-old friends. A generation X slacker film, it spoke to us – for us – at a time when we held dreams to change the world and had to face the reality of working crappy jobs to pay the rent. It could have starred most of the people I'd worked with at the cinema: actors, musicians, filmmakers, writers like me.

It centres on Winona Ryder's character. She's a valedictorian who wants to be a documentary maker and spends the film interviewing three friends about their dreams, hopes and loves. My nineties favourite, Janeane Garofalo, is one of the friends, with her usual quick-witted one-liners and sharp black fringe.

They chain-smoke like we did, visit 7-Eleven for munchies while stoned off their heads and dance to The Knack's 'My Sharona' like we did, visit grungy pubs to listen to a friend's band like we did, and have messy one-night stands and failed relationships like we did.

In the first few minutes of the film when Winona Ryder is interviewing Ethan Hawke for her documentary, he tells her that his dad is dying of prostate cancer.

My daughter and I cracked up laughing on the couch.

'Fuck, there are dead dads everywhere. You just can't escape them,' she says.

She was right. Half the films we'd watched in the past year had dead fathers, missing fathers, dying fathers or fathers who'd failed. Sure, dads die every day, but they seem to die in a rather disproportionate number in popular culture, almost like they are being used as a convenient narrative arc.

In *Reality Bites*, we never meet Ethan Hawke's father. He is an off-screen mention. A shitty dad who wasn't around and he dies towards the end of the film. But his death changes Ethan Hawke's character. Forces him to re-evaluate his choices. He comes back from Chicago wearing a suit and ready to commit to Winona Ryder. His father's death is a catalyst, a trope for change.

The dead-dad trope usually involves a father dying early in the film or sometimes even before the film starts. It loads emotional baggage onto the protagonist and gives them something to work through or to explain away their behaviour. There are many badly behaved dads in the Marvel Cinematic Universe. In fact, the argument has been made many a time that daddy issues provide the engine for all the stories.

Some of the heroes in the Marvel Cinematic Universe have two dead parents (Iron Man, Captain America, Spider-Man, Gamora and Scarlet Witch). Others have one, like Peter Quill and Black Panther. There are dead dads, dads who turn out not to be so great after all and, my personal favourite, evil dads like Thanos.

It would seem being a superhero requires having a tragic backstory.

I remember going to watch *Avengers: Endgame* just after Aidan was diagnosed. The four of us had bought tickets to a session on the opening day and we sat among a huge crowd of hardened fans. And then Tony Stark died and Aidan started crying in the seat next to me, as if he were watching his own death and the impact it would have on his children.

Classic books are even more dotted with deaths. Orphan stories like *Anne of Green Gables*, stories about friends dying like *Bridge to Terabithia*, the impending death of a mother in *A Monster Calls*, and who doesn't remember sobbing when Charlotte dies in *Charlotte's Web*.

My son has turned off films, stepped away from television and closed books that have introduced death as a subject. He wants to be entertained, not reminded.

But I am guilty of this too. In several of my middle-grade books, like *Sick Bay, The Secrets We Keep* and *The Jammer*, a character has a dead parent. With the exception of *The Jammer*, the books aren't about their deaths, but their deaths feature as part of the narrative. I started writing about death in my books because my mum had died and it was all I could see. I wrote to make sense of things, to process, because death is what I feared. But I never write about the character who is dying; it is always about the person left behind. Because that is what I've been. The one here after they are gone.

Perhaps that's what we are most afraid of. Being left. I know my son checks what time I'll be home more often than before, as if I might go out for dinner one night with friends and never return.

Two days before we were free to leave the house, something had shifted. Time had stretched and warped like it did in lockdown when nothing felt linear. That night, I fried prawns and my daughter and I ate them at the dining table, a half-completed jigsaw under our plates. We talked about philosophy and politics, about Aidan and his moods.

It was like being out with a friend. She could talk about most things: movies, books, the state of the world. As Aidan would say, 'She is fully cooked.'

The week was the longest time we'd spent together, just the two of us. With her brother isolating in his room and her dad gone, it was just her and me, cooking up vegetables for dinner, sharing a bag of caramel Easter eggs and watching all the films we had been meaning to see.

The two of us managed to escape Covid infection that time. And when my son re-emerged from his room at the end of the week, he brought with him all the whirling energy of someone who had missed company. He was ready to greet the world.

My daughter was the perfect companion, floating out for mealtimes and longer in the evenings and otherwise pottering in her room, singing Laura Marling songs and playing guitar. If she wasn't my daughter, I would happily share a house with her, but now she talks about wanting to fly. Tells me that she almost booked a ticket to Asia the other night and only stopped because she didn't have a credit card.

I'm both proud and grieving.

Scene Nine: This or Death

The day our daughter got her period for the first time, Aidan responded by letting her have the day off school and then rushing to the shops to buy her a bunch of pink carnations and a block of chocolate. She lay in bed with a cheeky grin and asked, 'Does this mean I can stay home from school every month?'

I envy her the openness she has about her body. My son too, laughing about the sprouting hair under his arms and the changes to his voice. A month or so before he died, Aidan sent me shopping with a list of things he wanted me to buy for our son: shaving cream, a razor and deodorant. Our son was twelve and laughed when his dad gave the presents to him, then he buried the presents in the bottom drawer of his desk. He's treasured them for three years now and uses them sparingly, like he is fearful of them running out.

★

I hated my body during those early teenage years and tried to hide it under layers of clothes. My parents were relaxed about nakedness, but I was permanently embarrassed.

I inherited Mum's weight obsession at an age when I went from being tall and naturally thin to having breasts and a bum and hating both. Mum had modelled before having me and I remember staring in wonder at the photographs of her in tiny sixties dresses, with a waist the size of a young child's. She was always on a diet: the Cottage Cheese, the Scarsdale, the Cabbage Soup.

My teenage diary has pages dedicated to lists of food with calories ingested, interspersed with lists of men I liked (with Tom Selleck at the top) and boys I liked (with the farmer's son occupying numbers one to three). It is a savage read, making me remember the torture of being that age.

The mid-eighties saw the rise of food and drink like Lean Cuisine and Diet Coke and an increased pressure to be thin. Aerobic gurus Jane Fonda and Richard Simmons plagued our television screens in flamboyant lycra and we swapped to low-fat everything. It wasn't overtly about starving yourself; it was often done under the guise of health. No more butter; margarine was better. At least we'd moved on from praying our weight away like Reverend Charlie W Shedd suggested in 1957, when he published his weight-loss journey, *Pray Your Weight Away*.

I still have *The Complete Scarsdale Medical Diet* book. A dull-looking thing with too much large type on the cover and a photograph of one of the authors, Dr Herman Tarnower. Published in the late seventies, the book became a bestseller when Tarnower was murdered by his jilted lover in 1980. Jean Harris was charged with second-degree murder and spent years in prison. Eleven years after her conviction, a new analysis of the shooting suggested there had been a struggle and Tarnower had tried to take the gun away, being shot in the process. Harris was released from prison on the evidence.

There were books written and films made, with references to Harris in *Seinfeld*, the film *Dolores Claiborne* and various songs. Nothing like a crime of passion to propel a fad diet to notoriety. At twelve, I knew none of this, just that Mum was convinced that two weeks on Scarsdale would help her to drop half a stone.

I have piles of photographs of Mum when she was young, her dark hair set in the fifties' style, wearing a slim-fit beaded dress and smiling at the camera.

Mum left school at fifteen. The second daughter of a single mother who'd been abandoned with three children when her husband fled to Papua New Guinea after the war to start a new family, Mum grew up in postwar public housing in Williamstown. With her mother working full-time and no boundaries, she spent her days roaming the rifle range, hiding behind the targets and escaping to the rooftops to read unseen.

As a child, I loved hearing her stories of the beetroot milkshakes she would make her friend down the road, pretending they were strawberry, or the dozen rationed eggs she cracked on the hot pavement to see if they would fry.

She was wild and hustled to get by. She learnt to sew young, so she could make her own clothes, and she entered a beauty contest to win enough money for a moped that she then drove without a licence and crashed. The first time she married was at eighteen to escape her life and she left him after a year. She was smart and kind and a keeper of secrets, and when she was young, she sometimes lived on nothing more than a banana and two Vita-Weat biscuits with a scraping of Vegemite.

Mum was a self-taught cook with real skills, but there were many days of eating dry pumpernickel bread and half a grapefruit, with a tub of lumpy spring-onion flavoured cottage cheese for dinner. Cottage cheese tastes just like I remember. And it takes me back to afternoons perched up at the long wooden bench of my childhood home, wishing I was chewing into a white-bread meatloaf sandwich with tomato sauce like my brother.

I have a bag of her clothes that I rescued from Dad's house after she died: a leather mini-dress with a zip down the front that I can't even slip over my shoulders, a designer-made flamenco number with a plunging neckline and folds of coloured ruffles that drop to the ground, and her white raw-silk wedding dress, which she made herself, that looks like it might fit me if I had all my ribs removed.

She was obsessed with staying slim. It was an unspoken competitive sport between her and her friends. When Mum was diagnosed with cancer and started her chemotherapy treatment, she stopped eating. She couldn't stomach anything and she began losing weight. We went shopping one day and she tried on a coloured stretch-cotton dress. She bought it because it was a size eight and she hadn't worn anything that small for years.

I kept that dress. Unworn, it still has the tag hanging from the label at the neck.

I remember my shock at seeing my mum change into bathers when she was about the age I am now, her body not dissimilar to

Act Three: Other Scenes

my own: sagging breasts and puckered skin from stretch marks across my hips. But I try not to look away at my own. Not like I did when I saw Mum in the change room that day.

Each week now there is something different going on in my body: itchy skin, foggy brain, sore shoulder, creaking knees, the beginning of arthritis in my knuckles. And just as I begin to accept each new sensation, it leaves, only to be replaced by another.

My conversations with friends begin with a round-up of complaints. It's all so uncertain. Some women sail through menopause, others suffer for years. Nobody has definitive answers, and just like those wobbly beginnings of periods starting and breast buds appearing apparently overnight, we are back to feeling at odds with our bodies.

Possibly in reaction to watching Aidan die, I have decided to test my body out, setting it little challenges. Can I run five kilometres when I haven't run for ten years? Can I rollerskate with my roller-derby-playing son for an hour? Can I do a handstand against a wall without crumpling?

The answer is not gracefully, not expertly and certainly not very well. My run is more of a shuffle Cliff-Young-in-gumboots style. My rollerskating is helped by clutching at the carpeted wall. And my handstand is a hand-lean, where my feet touch the wall at an angle.

But I don't want to stop. I want to see what I can do in this ageing shell, in this almost-menopausal body that likes to respond by hurting me.

My right shoulder hasn't been the same since I attempted an assisted chin-up, my left knee became inflamed during the 2020 lockdowns when I kicked a soccer ball to my son and had to hobble up the stairs for months afterwards, my right eye is often red and inflamed and nobody knows why, but my brother affectionately calls it Cheezel eye because it looks just like it did when he tried to throw a Cheezel in my mouth as a kid and missed. Instead, it collided with my eye, causing it to be red for days.

I talk to someone in my apartment block about feeling tired, and he says, quite rightly, 'We can whinge, but it's either this or death.'

This or death. My new motto.

In 2019, about a year before the pandemic hit, when things were hard in our house, I joined a gym. It's fifty metres from my house so I can't use distance as an excuse not to go. It's a lovely space, pastel painted walls and big industrial windows. The bathroom has drawers of tampons that I rarely need now, and hair ties and hair clips, and sometimes chocolate, and there is always a pot of spiced cinnamon tea that you can drink before you start your class.

Here, I've learnt how to bench press, how to deadlift, how to squat and how to box. I surprise myself that I keep turning up, but I do. It's one of the few regular things in my life, the only place I must be. Now I go four times a week, sometimes five. There are classes I particularly like because the instructors are young and funny and they have playlists full of music that I listened to when I was young and funny. Playlists of songs they were not born for the first time round.

Most classes, I disappear into menopausal brain fog when the instructor is explaining the exercise, so invariably I must ask them to show me again how to do something. I can never lift the heaviest weights or pull off the lowest squat or even properly stretch at the end, but it's not that sort of place. It's not competitive.

I'm often the oldest in the room. Unless my friend is with me, but she's a year younger anyway. I'm old enough to be a mother to most of the other people who come, but strangely that doesn't bother me. I still pull my hair into a ponytail, wear second-hand gym pants and a t-shirt that once belonged to Aidan, and mostly manage to keep up.

My friend and I joke about the guns we're going to have one day, which we both know will never happen. But I can feel the slight rise of muscle on my upper arms and the ease of dashing up the stairs without my calves hurting. And that is something.

This or death.

Until now, my body has mostly changed without my input. It has changed through puberty and pregnancy, through ageing and nature. But now there are little changes caused by my own will. I can make it move faster, lift heavier, squat lower and stand longer on one leg. And with each little change, I feel a connection to my body that I haven't felt in a long time.

When I was thirteen, I played netball and tennis, swam laps and ran for fun. At the time I might have said I exercised because I liked competition, being with my friends or because I had a crush on someone in the team. But now I know that exercise for me is not about any of those things (although I do love the morning chats with my friend at the gym). Exercise is partly about leaving my thoughts. I'm no longer just a head on legs. I'm connected to muscles and joints. I'll never be able to achieve the perfect burpee or run a marathon, but I don't care. I just want to stop thinking for an hour and move.

Being a writer is tiring because when you aren't writing, you're thinking about writing or wondering how you will possibly make it through another winter without a real job. Particularly when there's a low-level anxious drone in your brain about money and bills and illness and mortality and the children and the state of the world and anything else I can find to make me worry. I like having a break from that and instead starting my morning with the simple act of sweating.

But the main reason I've become a fan of exercise is that now when my body hurts, it's not just because of age, but because I have caused it. Because I have woken sleeping muscles up with unfamiliar movements. That is the joy for me of exercising. That I now ache because of something that I did.

It's this or death.

Scene Ten: Birthday

It's six days before my daughter's eighteenth birthday. I've been stressing over the perfect present for months now, alternating between artwork and jewellery. Something that will last. But she already wears fingers full of rings and her walls are covered with posters of obscure arthouse films and black-and-white photographs of her dad and me when we were young.

And then when I was trying to sleep, I had a thought. One of those drowsy moments of brilliance. I would buy her a second-hand piano. One that can live in our apartment until she moves it into her own place. A present that will lure her back, bringing her home to play.

She hasn't even left yet, but already I'm dreading the day when I know she will.

Years ago, I had promised to buy her a piano when our friends returned from overseas and reclaimed theirs. But we were renting and I didn't want to move something so large each time we found a new place to live.

That promise became one of many that I've made as a parent, one I always fully intended to deliver on, but one I also knew was buying me time. Now it seems like just the right object that will symbolise everything I want to say to her.

I learnt to play on a 1970s Yamaha keyboard when I was a kid and can remember 'Every Good Boy Deserves Fruit' as the way to pick out notes. Nothing else has stuck though, so I ring my friend, who is a classical pianist, for advice. Within an hour, we have sourced a recently listed Kawai model on Facebook Marketplace for six hundred dollars. My friend says it's a bargain and tells me to go and look at it immediately. I message the owner and jump in the car.

It's Sunday and there's little traffic. I drive across town to an area I only visit when my son and I are on an op-shopping spree – the stretch of bayside suburbs where teenagers learn to drive in cars that cost more than my annual salary.

I pull up outside a house. It's all sharp lines and edges. The gate is locked and it takes me a minute or two to notice a panel of buttons. I slide my reading glasses onto my face so that I can find the buzzer to press and look at what I assume is a camera.

I wonder what they see: unbrushed and unwashed hair, greying at the roots, no make-up, clothes that need a clean. Clearly, an imposter. I fight this feeling of not belonging, but it flares up when I'm in rich streets with houses that I clearly cannot afford.

The gate opens automatically and I walk up the footpath made of smooth white stones. The front door swings wide before I reach it. A woman is peering at me. We're about the same age, but she's fit-looking and lean, dressed in running clothes. A jumpy, squat white dog sniffs my crotch and the woman calls it off.

I follow her inside, thinking for a second how trusting it is to enter a stranger's house to buy something you've found on the internet. Particularly when I'm doing it alone. I should have dragged my son with me as back-up.

But the thought leaves me when I see the piano in the corner of the white room. She tells me it is a 1972 Japanese-made darkwood upright piano. I am instantly in love. Cannot take my eyes off it. And then I notice that there is no clutter, no piles of teetering junk. I'm jealous for a second, thinking about my apartment where stuff leaks from drawers and shelves, where dirty socks stay in the hallway for a day or two until someone finally picks them up and tosses them in the direction of the laundry.

The woman tells me I can play the piano to see if I like it. She lifts the cover and removes a long strip of red felt placed over the keys to keep them clean. I know that will be the first thing to go in our house.

I sit down on the hard wooden stool and press each of the blacks and the whites tentatively. But I feel like a fraud, not knowing one tone from another. Embarrassed, I explain it is going to be my daughter's eighteenth birthday present, and we talk a little about our children. She tells me the piano has been hers since she was a child and they've kept it in the family, but nobody plays it anymore.

I talk too much, a habit I keep intending to change, but one that always returns when I'm most uncomfortable. She asks me what school my children attend and I tell her. I don't reciprocate. I don't know why it matters.

Stuck for anything else to say, I buy the piano within minutes, transferring the money on the spot and telling her I'll find someone to collect it later in the week. Now that I've decided to take it, I just want to leave.

I'm outside again, opening the gate before I even know what's happened. I'm not an impulsive person and I often miss out on things because I take too long to consider all the angles, so I'm not sure what it is about the piano that lured me into such a fast sale.

Driving home, I stop at an upmarket grocery store and buy bagels and a drink. I start thinking about the piano, hoping I've done the right thing. I don't even know if it is any good or if my daughter will like the lean, mid-century look or would prefer an older, more traditional model.

The drive home is slower, giving me time to think, time to worry some more.

I cross the river that divides our city, leaving behind the leafy suburbs by the beach and heading for the graffiti and treeless stretches in the inner north where we live. There's been a battle over rubbish recently and the garbage removalists are currently on strike, demanding higher wages. The council bins ooze onto the road and there's a certain smell in the air.

When we first moved here more than twenty years ago, it was cheap to rent and full of Italian and Greek families with vegie patches and chickens in their backyards. Like all the inner-city suburbs, it has been gentrified. There are more bike shops, record stores and music studios than before. Vegans are a dime a dozen. But the essence of the suburb has remained: a left-wing stronghold full of artists and people seeking community.

There are sometimes fights at night on the busy main streets.

Act Three: Other Scenes

Car horns toot. A beer bottle is often tucked behind a back wheel of my car from some late-night partygoers playing a trick. We chat to neighbours in the street and see our friends who live close enough to reach on foot or on bike. The kids walk to school with the same kids they've known since they were little. Someone drops off eggs from their fast-laying chicken. Herbs grow in cracks in the laneways if you know where to look.

Sometimes I feel boxed in, trapped by the high-rise apartment blocks and the traffic that moves at a snail's pace. But today, I feel relieved to be back on my side of the city. Somewhere I can shop in my pyjamas and wear the same black jeans for a week.

I find a pile of letters my daughter wrote to the fairies. She used to write each night and Aidan and I would take it in turns to respond. Sometimes we'd forget and one of us would elbow the other in bed late at night, hoping enough short stabs in the ribs would make the other get up and write a reply.

Aidan was more inventive than I was. His contributions were things like words spelt out in small pebbles on the back step or petals in a love-heart shape. I always scribbled notes, sometimes remembering to mask my handwriting because she was a smart detective, even at six.

The Irish comedian and writer Spike Milligan used to leave fairy letters for his daughters too – delicate writings with tiny stamps left for them to find around the garden and the house. Our letters were never as beautiful as Spike's, but they had the same intention: to create magic, to create conversation, to suspend disbelief.

It doesn't seem like twelve years since we wrote those letters. So much of parenting young children is waiting for them to grow. And so much of parenting older children is wishing they hadn't.

It's been twenty-three months since Aidan died. Many of them spent in lockdowns where we couldn't try out our new family in public. Now we are back in the world and it's not just me who's changed. My son has stepped cautiously into the space his dad has left. He towers over me, sometimes protective, and I find myself torn between liking this new grown-up version of him and wanting the child version to return. My daughter is wary, sometimes distant. She went into the first lockdown at fifteen with a curfew and a father who was still mobile and came out the other end nearly an adult, with no dad and unlimited freedom.

The three of us are at times unified. And at others the gap of him looms large.

Sometimes I feel it's me who is in the way of the two teenagers bonding over a shared knowledge of teachers and school, laughing about things I know nothing about. And I'm steps behind, trying to catch up, trying to force my way into the line-up so they remember me.

Sometimes over dinner when I'm hassling one of them about something or being generally argumentative, I catch them sharing a look that makes me feel like an outlier. I lack that other person to rant with. The second adult who has my back. And I wonder if my singleness makes them keener to leave.

Act Three: Other Scenes

I find myself yearning to be back in those newborn and toddler days when I had the two of them at home with me, one in a sling and one chattering her way around the house beside me. When I was at the centre.

Now I'm watching them grow. I'm watching them step free of grief and prepare to re-enter the world, leaving me behind with my memories. My daughter is saving for the day she can leave home and I am training myself to nod and smile and find something supportive to offer when, inside, all of me is screaming *no*.

I can't lose another one.

When we first tottered out of our final lockdown in 2021, I kept her close, restricting socialising, collecting her from parties, keeping tabs. She was frustrated by me. And then she said one night that her friend had told her she should understand because I'd already lost Aidan and I was making sure she was safe. Embarrassed at how obvious it was to her teenage friend, I stopped hovering and gave her space.

For days I tease my daughter about her present, letting her guess and second-guess her guesses. She loves a secret, but she wants to know.

On the day before her birthday while she is at school, the piano delivery person I've booked uses a small custom-built wooden trolley to wheel the piano into our apartment. He upsells me on some wooden discs to place under the legs to protect our floors. I'm an easy target and would agree to anything, wanting the birthday present to be just right.

We talk music and instruments, and he likes that our place

is full of drum kits and guitars. He tells me the piano is a real beauty, in great condition and a rare find these days. He tells me it is worth much more than I paid and that I should never sell it.

I respond by covering it in blankets and pillows, trying to disguise its shape which, of course, is never going to work because it still looks like a piano covered in blankets and pillows.

All afternoon, I have that satisfied smug feeling, like I've pulled off a heist, successfully purchasing the ultimate present that will prove my worth as a parent.

When my daughter comes home with her boyfriend, she squeals at the shape, begging me to be allowed to pull the blankets off. I unveil it with a theatrical flourish and she throws herself down to play. It is loud and lovely hearing that sound that I've missed.

She wraps her arms around me, disbelieving that it is hers. I don't usually spend so much money on my children's presents, but there is an importance to her eighteenth birthday that I've never experienced before.

Even her fourteen-year-old brother seems aware of it as he makes her a card with a sketch of her face and the words: *Please don't leave. If you want to move out, come and live on my floor.* It breaks me that he feels like that. That he too senses the weight of this shrinking family.

It's not just her impending adulthood that is rocking us. It's the changes in her. The leaving behind of the sweet crushes on various actors and countless indie singers, and the beginning of a relationship with, in Pinocchio's words, a 'real boy'. A real boy who stays the night and makes her laugh and brings his dishes to the sink from the table. A real boy who leaves clothes in our

Act Three: Other Scenes

house for the next time and buys board games for us to play as a family. This real boy has almost redressed the balance and filled the male side of the seesaw.

And I can't help but wonder what her dad would have thought.

As unspoken compensation for all that she has lost, we plan three events for her birthday. I never admit it is the reason for my generosity, just that I want it to be special, as if plying her with presents and parties will patch over all the loss of the past two years.

I've become very skilled at pretending.

She throws herself a party with friends at our place while I am away, leaving notes to prepare the neighbours and ditching all the bottles before I come home. She even cleans the floors, although I do need to run the mop across missed patches and sticky corners.

The second party is with our family and her boyfriend at the restaurant down the road on the actual day. I'm acting at being a grown-up with a salary and I tell everyone I will pay and then must swallow my shame as I have to transfer money from my kids' accounts to cover the costs, promising to pay them back when I can.

The last party is a borrowed idea from a friend with older children who marked their entrance to adulthood with a gathering of close friends. My daughter writes the guest list and I send the messages, inviting a small circle of people who have watched her grow.

We take my daughter's first legal trip to the bottle shop to stock up. She is ready to flash her learner's permit to show anyone asking that she is allowed to be here, but nobody does.

We find a trolley and load it full of prosecco. I let her choose. She picks the bottles with the prettiest labels and the cheapest price. I talk her into some of those on the next shelf up, explaining that we can spend a bit more. I even offer to buy something French. Something fancy. Instead, she rushes around trying to find some Korean sweet wine she drinks at parties with friends. They've been drinking it for a while now. High in alcohol content, it does the job. They buy it at the Asian grocer where nobody asks for ID and it costs next to nothing.

She is disappointed when she can't find what she is looking for. Tells me she doesn't like the taste of alcohol. Only drinks it when she wants to feel the effect. I sort of understand. It takes me back to the Island Coolers I drank as a sixteen-year-old and makes her seem like my child again, not like the adult she is fast becoming.

We pay and it comes to hundreds. She looks shocked, knowing that it is a lot of money for me to spend on entertaining old family friends. We stack the bottles into the back of the car, laughing at the sound of clinking glass as we drive off and turn the corner. I tell her what I am cooking and we do a supermarket shop on the way home, buying bags of potato chips and a long list of ingredients.

I spend hours making cakes and sausage rolls and rolling arancini balls in my hands. The house fills with the smell of stinky overripe cheese and garlic.

The buzzer sounds and a steady stream of guests arrive. It is still technically winter, but we open windows because of the warmth of all the bodies. My friend takes over cooking the arancini balls in hot oil, frying them gently, because I start in a frenzy and mess up the first batch. He wears my apron. The one I bought from a school fete many years ago. The one I never wear because I can never be bothered dragging it from the drawer.

We show off our apartment, this place we've finally made ours. The cat hides in my room, cowering under the bed, until my friend's daughter joins her and they sit together on my rarely made bed playing a video game.

Presents are given and pile up, and prosecco is opened and finished and opened and finished. My son drinks all the soft drink when he thinks I'm not watching and hangs out in his room with two of his friends, eating cake and olives and playing old vinyl on his record player. My daughter chats, proving her grown-up ways. She is gracious and graceful and nothing like me. I am loud and sweary and forget to ask questions. She listens. She nods. She impresses me.

I must stop myself from crying. She is an adult now with only one parent.

A friend brings a little tub of glitter and spills it everywhere: on the floor and the chairs and the cat's paws. Tiny shards of sparkles that we will probably have to sweep up for days.

I improvise a terrible speech and we sing happy birthday. I cut the passionfruit sponge I made that is leaning to one side and the cheesecake my friend made that isn't.

Another hour passes and all that is left is the stinky cheese and half a bottle of white wine. People start leaving, drifting out to the rest of their Sundays. A couple stays and he plays the piano, bringing it to life under his hands. It is festive and too loud for our apartment, but I don't care. The sound takes me back to when my daughter was little, to when I was enough.

She sits on the floor and opens her presents and I think how like her father she is – waiting until people have gone so she can operate in private and thank them properly when she has time.

He is missed. But he is here too. In the people we love. In the friends who knew him best. In my kids. In my efforts to sweep the floor and do a quick 'whip round', his favourite expression. In my spending too much money on my daughter's birthday to make it special without him.

By eight we are all in bed. Exhausted. Too tired to talk about him. Too tired to say what we are all feeling. That things are different now.

A couple of weeks later and it is Father's Day and our house is unusually quiet. If Aidan was here, it would have meant coffee in bed and cards drawn by hand. Nothing much. Simple really. But now the kids have nowhere to send those feelings.

They are in their rooms. I am in the lounge. It is only the sound of the cat galloping up and down the polished floorboards that marks time. When she is hungry, she reaches up to scratch my arm as if reminding me that it is my job to feed her.

We collectively hate Father's Day, but we lack the energy to come together and commiserate.

We are separate, scattered into our thoughts, our memories.

Sometime in the afternoon, after a scavenged lunch of bits and bobs retrieved from the kitchen and taken back to rooms to eat, my daughter ventures out. She asks if she can play and I shrug because I want to say no, but I don't have the heart to stop her. And she sits down at the piano, plays an Elton John song and sings along. I listen for a minute or two, her voice strong and melodic.

Act Three: Other Scenes

And then, for no discernible reason, it is the thing that makes me teary, and I leave the room for the toilet, staying there until she's finished.

She comes and finds me later, telling me she might move out next year into a share house. I stop myself from crying again. Instead, I ask if we should find a piano tuner and we discuss that for a minute, safely back on solid ground. I am not up to talking about the endless permutations of her leaving.

Before Covid, when my daughter was only fifteen, I would wait up and collect her from whatever party she was at. I'd drive home a collection of kids, listening mainly to their chatter in the car, enjoying their energy. Now she has friends who drive. Friends who can buy alcohol legally. Friends whose names I do not know.

We are close still – the hug she needs when she's had a fight with someone, the conversation about philosophy that she is happy to share, tells me so. I ache when I see her. Grown and fatherless. Wondering how she will find herself in the world now that she has known such grief.

I bravely mention Father's Day and ask if she's okay. Without answering, she tells me about one of her friends who is driving around Melbourne, dropping off chocolate and flowers to everyone he knows who finds Father's Day hard: a couple of boys who don't see their dads and three girls still mourning theirs.

I fight the tears again. And hold them back until she walks out of the room.

And as she sits down at the piano and plays, I let the tears roll.

Scene Eleven: Grass Widow

On Sundays, I often find myself feeling jealous of the cat, who instinctively knows how to get what she wants. If she's hungry, she circles my legs, following me from one room to the next, until I inevitably surrender and fill her bowl. If she wants her litter tray emptied, she whines at me until I stop whatever I'm doing and scoop out the poo. And it's not just me who does her bidding. While the kids keep their doors shut to me, she finds a way in, sleeping on their beds, curling up on their laps, being patted and adored. I have considered kneeling and scratching at their paintwork until they let me in too, but I can't imagine it would be met with the same tenderness.

On weekdays, I can almost forget that Aidan won't be home later, cleaning the kitchen or prepping dinner. During the week, my days are busy with work and washing, cooking, shopping, life. I am the same as the next person, competing in snatches of conversation for who has the least free time. And on Saturday nights, I can often rustle up something to do: a dinner or a drink, or a movie on the couch with my son.

But on Sundays, once a sacred day, I am lost. There's a hard edge to me that doesn't soften until Monday comes. It's the day when the rest of my world seems busy, pottering at home with a partner to fill the gaps, sleeping in with a partner to bring them tea, heading down the street for the weekly shop with a partner to help them carry it all home. I know this is untrue because not all my friends are partnered, through choice or circumstance, but when I'm flat, I believe I am the only one.

In the past, I would have rallied Aidan and the kids and dragged them to a park for a walk or a kick of a ball. Perhaps I would have suggested a trip to the country for scones or a visit to the gallery for some culture. Now I must pick my words carefully, crafting my offers with a dangled carrot that will appeal.

I might still be able to tempt my son to an early morning visit to Camberwell Market, knowing that as soon as we arrive, he will wander one way and I will go another, meeting up for a doughnut at the end. But at least we have the drive there and back. Trapped together, seatbelts on, we might chat about school or friends or something random, his words filling my day.

My daughter is rarely home now on a Sunday morning, or if she is, she's asleep. Her Sundays are full of friends, of gigs and dinners, of dates and conversation.

On the worst Sundays, I pick fights. Petty and mean. If the kids retreat to their rooms, wisely avoiding me, I circle after them, pushing and niggling until one of them snaps and I walk away, feeling injured.

It's only later when I start to cry in my room on my own that I realise it's that mass of grief that builds and only bursts when I crack. The next day it will be gone and I'll forget for a bit, until it hovers again, changing me for a few hours into someone I don't always recognise.

Perhaps it is no coincidence that given Aidan died on a Sunday, that is the day of the week I struggle with most. It's the day that reminds me that he's gone. Perhaps there is something about the rhythm of it that takes me back.

I find myself watching young families out on the streets, aware that I'm looking to the past for the children mine once were, when Sundays meant a sleep-in until seven am, if we were lucky, and then breakfast at the table before hours of Lego or drawing or making cakes. Those days where their worlds were no bigger than our house, where the tail of the weekend meant just us.

After Aidan died, I filled my days, knowing the loneliness that would creep in without him. I am careful not to want my children to look after me. I do not want them stepping into that space where Aidan once stood, but I know it happens sometimes because the diminishing size of our family now means that roles are more fluid – my daughter parenting her younger brother, me spilling secrets to my daughter that I would have spilt to Aidan, my son and I sharing the couch like an old couple on a Saturday night.

I must stay the parent.

When my daughter tells me she worries about me because I don't have the joy of planning things with my partner anymore, like she now does, she is quick to add that she doesn't pity me.

Act Three: Other Scenes

And I'm quicker to reassure. To point out that she is in the first flush of love and I am out the other end, knowing that even if he was here, we wouldn't plan in the same way.

I'm touched that she thinks about me and my loneliness.

I tell her that it's okay. It's only on a Sunday.

But that's not always true. I miss him on other days too. Days when I just want to talk, when I want to share some news, when I must step into an unfamiliar role.

On a day when three young electricians are fitting a ceiling fan above our dining table, I hide in my room with the cat. The men are loud and tattooed, strong and confident in their words to me. I hear myself apologising for the state of the place as they enter, my words tumbling out in bursts. 'It's a mess, sorry.' Like they care, like they even notice, like I'm anything but another job.

My son comes to say goodbye before heading to school and whispers his amusement.

'G'day, mate,' he says, gripping my hand in a pretend shake, mimicking what has just been said to him.

My daughter just ignores them – wafts through with her long dress and her perfumed air.

It's not the men we are thrown by. They are polite, professional, respectful. It is us. This new unsettled three, trying to make sense of the world now that Aidan has gone.

Aidan would have dealt with this. With the men.

One of the young men, perhaps his name is Brodie, peeps around my door to ask a question. I follow him out, aware that I'm still in morning clothes, things I'd grabbed from the floor.

I reach the dining room where the men are up ladders, looking down. One makes a joke, friendly, but I don't quite laugh.

The dark-haired one wants to know if I want the fan slightly to the left or to the right.

'Honestly, I don't care,' I tell him.

He nods like he understands and suggests the right might be best. I shrug and head back to my room.

There is drilling as they reach into the roof to fit the motor. The cat stretches and sighs on my bed like she's heard it all before. I try to watch the UK crime show that I didn't manage to finish the night before, headphones in to keep the sound of the men out.

The drilling stops and one of my ear buds drops. I hear laughter and the movement of ladders.

The cat leaves me to investigate and I wonder what she'll find.

The men have finished. The fan is spinning.

One of them tells me, 'It's a good one. Not going to break,' like he wants me to know that I've chosen well.

He hands me the remote and explains how to use it, apologises for not screwing it into the wall but they don't do that job.

I tell him, 'I'll use double-sided tape.'

He grins. Asks me if one of the other guys told me to do that.

'No. I worked it out myself,' I tell him.

'Cool,' he says. And because I'm desperate to be more than I am, I point out the spikes on the outside air-conditioning unit that are secured with double-sided tape to scare away the nesting pigeons and pretend I climbed up all that way to secure them. I don't tell him that it was a man who did it. A friend who worked out a way to deter the pigeons from their nightly visits where they pooed and pooed and pooed.

Act Three: Other Scenes

I let him think that I too am unafraid of a ladder.

Brodie sweeps up the dust from the drilling and leaves it in little piles around the room. He tries to take an old iPhone and charger from the floor, thinking they are his.

I snatch them back. It's Aidan's old phone. I've been trying to get it to turn on so I can read messages. From me to him. From before.

They carry their three matching ladders to the door. One of them stops to pat the cat and she surprises me by allowing it.

The man looks up and tells me he has two of his own. He has a tattoo on his calf that stretches as he does. And I turn away from the ladders and the men as they go.

In the block of apartments that we now live in, I am surrounded by women living alone.

One owns a greyhound, saved from a post-racing death, that wears booties to protect its paws from glass. A ceramicist by trade, she still wears her love of art in the way she enquires about my writing. I like her enormously. My son does too. He stops to chat to her about pottery and craft. They share a love of found objects and collections.

Another walks her small dog through the car park and she stops to chat to me about grief, wading right into the hard subjects like loss and moving on. She is warm and funny and tells me I'm welcome to come and drink wine and watch *Married at First Sight* if I ever need company. It's her guilty pleasure, she says with a laugh.

My friend's mum, who lives upstairs from me, sometimes drops in with plates of warm homemade food: stuffed peppers and bags full of dolmades and börek. I cannot explain how happy I am to receive these foods. With Aidan and Mum both gone, the arrival of meals is a treat. It means someone is looking out for me.

These women are me in twenty years or so, carving out space and living alone. They are smart and lively and independent. Sometimes one of the kids comments on it too, that here in the apartment building, at least I'll have people to talk to.

I just hope they don't leave me all alone with the cat anytime soon.

I am alone, yes, but not a widow. Aidan and I weren't married. So, now I'm just single. Again. After twenty-five years, I became single days before turning fifty, at the tail end of the long Melbourne winter lockdown, when I cut my own hair, stopped getting dressed every day and ate my sadness.

Perhaps I am a 'grass widow': I am an unmarried woman with children who pretends to have been married, but never was. Although this term is now used to mean a woman whose husband has left, for work or through divorce or separation.

In German the term is *Strohwitwe*, meaning straw widow, a temporary state of loneliness. Dating back to 1399, women who had lost their virginity before their wedding were made to wear a straw wreath, marking them as a *Strohwitwe*.

I prefer the addition of the grass, which suggests life and freshness, rather than straw, which sounds dry and hard and uncomfortable. In English, it changed to grass in the 1500s, but the term had the same meaning: either a woman who had lost her virginity before the wedding or was a deserted mistress.

Act Three: Other Scenes

It was simple when Aidan was alive to call him my partner. But now he is dead, what do I say? Institutions remain conventional places and I find myself receiving condolences for the death of my husband each time I phone to sort out a bill.

He was not … I want to say but understand it will further confuse them.

Aidan asked me to marry him three times in our years together: once when he was drunk from the back seat of a car as a friend drove us home for a dinner party, once when we were walking home late in the rain and once after one of his brothers had just died.

It was not hard to refuse these proposals. I had no interest in being married. I did like the idea of a large and wild party with all our friends, but we couldn't afford one, so the wedding part seemed pointless. Besides, I didn't really believe his proposals because he didn't want to be married any more than I did.

I am no longer somebody's partner. I am floating alone. There is a weight in claiming marriage when you face the world and most people assumed we were married anyway, but that frustrates me too. Never being married makes it hard to explain my loss to people. It makes no difference legally, but it makes a difference to how I think about myself.

I want my position known and understood, but I want it to mean the same thing as if we'd taken vows.

In Joyce Carol Oates's essay 'A Widow's Story', published in *The New Yorker* after her husband's death from an infection in his lung, and taken from her lengthy memoir published in 2011, she talks about collecting his things from the hospital as her first job after her husband has died. His death is sudden and nothing like Aidan's, but I find myself being entranced by her description of 'pre-widowhood', the stage before the widow understands what is about to happen to them. She talks about the 'small tasks' that can bring the widow comfort, tasks I could not access for we were trapped in a pandemic and all the usual rituals and requirements were not on offer.

Perhaps this is why we love a funeral, because it is a focus for our attention now that the real work of grief is about to begin. I made lists after Aidan died. Managed my feelings with task administration, cancelling accounts, answering messages – anything to delay the pain I knew was coming.

In the essay, Oates talks about her long marriage to Raymond and about how in a marriage you always assume you have time – time for the conversations you haven't yet had. Perhaps that explains why Aidan and I didn't talk about much in those months where all we had was time. And that when he died there was a sense that we'd only just begun.

Aidan's most successful play, *The Architect*, was an examination of dying, finished when he knew his cancer was terminal. I have re-read the play many times since he died, looking for clues, hunting for suggestions that he was more at peace than he appeared.

This is a speech from towards the end of the play when the protagonist, Helen, is farewelling those she loves:

And I will die here with the people I love. Surrounded by the people I love … And I will not be gone. Try as you might, you won't be rid of me just yet. But you are the ones who possess me now. With remembrances. Here and there. A photograph. A song. A book. A flower in the garden. I'll be here for a while yet in every vacant moment ... but please let me go in time. In time ... Until then ... I'm just in the other room. For as long as you need me ...

Aidan was in the other room. People always are when they are dying. Already a step out of reach of us, in a room we can't fully access. That is when the loneliness starts. Not when they die, but when they are going to. That's the point of separation. Even in the closest of unions, married or not, it is hard to be in the same room when one of us is about to die.

Perhaps I expected Aidan to be as eloquent with his death as he was with his characters. Perhaps I thought we too would have speeches worthy of transcribing. We did not. It was all pain management, coffee consumption and sadness. His close friends wrote him letters that he did not respond to. I asked him questions that he left unanswered.

In Oates's essay, she talks about the visits to the hospital as her husband is moved from one ward to another, his condition worsening as the doctors find something else wrong. We had no hospital time. Just home time where I played doctor and nurse.

I find myself feeling envious of Oates's experience – her visits to the hospital where she could arrive fresh and worried, taking a seat beside her husband's bed, holding his hand and just loving him. When someone dies, we think about how it could have been done better. I made mistakes. I didn't say the right things even when we had time; but even if I had, he still would have died and I would still be lonely.

When I meet widows about my age we bond quickly over shared experiences of grief. There are jokes about the endless trays of lasagnes that lined our freezers, the flowers that filled our houses and the exhaustion of parenting children alone. And there is a shorthand that comes with meeting others who have been through it too. A sort of insider knowledge I'm sure we all wish we didn't have.

Sometimes I find myself deliberately leaving dirty dishes in the sink, bandaid wrappers beside the bed, the same plant unwatered. I think I might be waiting to see if anyone else will notice. Aidan would have. But the kids are skilled at stepping over most things, not seeing the ground or the dust or the cat hair that swirls in clumps near the edges of doorways. They don't move the dishes in the sink or water the sagging plant.

It's like I'm waiting for him to come back.

Scene Twelve: Single

As a child, I loved nothing more than a glimpse of my parents' adult lives. Now as an adult, I long for access to the worlds of my children. Since Aidan died, I have noticed a coming together of the old and the young in my life. My children know my friends and I know theirs, and the boundaries between us are increasingly blurred. I'm not sure if this is a common happening for single parents, or if the shift has occurred because we are a smaller unit than we once were so we look for extras, or if it is the community rallying around us, forming a circle to help us heal.

When I host dinner parties now, I go to double the effort, like I'm making up for Aidan not being there. The last one I threw, I cooked too much food and fussed around for too long in the kitchen, wanting to prove myself, wanting to impress. If Aidan had been with us, he would have washed all the glasses before the guests arrived. He would have set the table with his hospitality flair and picked out a record to set the mood. And when our friends arrived, our kids probably would have said hello, been polite, and then grabbed a plate of dinner and scurried away to their rooms.

But on this occasion, with Aidan missing and me alone, they both chose to stay. They sat at the table, ate dinner with the adults, made conversation, laughed. Our daughter drank a glass of wine and then, surprising all of us, cancelled her plans so she could remain where she was for the rest of the evening. It was joyful having them there, watching them both chat easily to people they had known half their lives. People who had known their dad, people who had fed them when he was dying, hugged them when he died, and cared for them as they grieved and grew.

I like to think that it's not just because our apartment is small that we are so intertwined in each other's lives. I like to think it is because we all want it this way.

There is an age that your children reach where you are less instrumental in parenting and more in just being present. It's the sweet spot, where your children know you as something other than belonging to them, when they are curious about the existence of your world outside theirs and when you can enjoy each other away from setting boundaries. Okay, so they might still forget to ask questions about your day but, if prompted, they are interested.

Now when my daughter's friends come, a magical bunch of new adults in their second-hand clothes and chunky boots, their home-cut fringes and newly learnt skills, they sit around Aidan's childhood table and chat. They cook for me and I for them and it is freeing to have this energy in our apartment. I wander through, joining them for a time. They are frank and wise, impressive in their ability to meet my gaze and treat me the way they would any other. I don't feel like I must shield them from the adult I was, picking out conversation carefully so as not to reveal too much of myself. I am mostly just me.

After I first had a baby, there were so many conversations with women friends about wishing we'd known more so we could have been better prepared. I am glad I didn't know more about this phase of parenting. This gathering up of time, when children age faster than they did at the beginning and tower over you, making you feel small in their hugs. It has been a great wonder discovering this end, the pause before they leave, the joy of our places becoming more equal.

Perhaps, too, I parent differently now that Aidan is gone. I'm looser because it's just me. I don't have to negotiate with him if we don't agree. I call all the shots. I still make dinners, cook vegetables each day, tell my son to go to sleep and wake him up for school. I am still there for late-night tears or advice about jobs or friends or the future but, more and more, I am unrequired.

Soon I will not be needed very often at all.

I am trying to see this as liberation and not as a stage to mourn. I am trying to celebrate their independence, their courage, their freedoms, knowing my own independence, courage and freedoms are about to return too.

One night, I'm invited via text to drinks at the rooftop of a nearby pub. Friends are already there. It's a last-minute thing. I dress in the cleanest clothes I can find, excited at the thought of getting out and relieved that the drinks are early so I can tell my son I'll be home for dinner. My social life is contained to short bursts where I can be home for him if his sister is out. I don't like leaving him alone late into the night.

My daughter has drawers of make-up that I raid sometimes. It used to be the other way round and for a second I wonder when it switched. It seems I wasn't paying attention. I dig out a lipstick. It's pale and pink, not red like I would have once worn. I swipe the colour across my mouth and check my face in her mirror. There are new lines etched into my neck and jaw that weren't there the last time I looked.

I pocket the lipstick for later, reminding myself to tell her I borrowed it.

The fastest way to the bar is the little gap between the fence and the medical centre, down the lane I only travel when it's still light. The fence is covered with posters advertising some band or another. Most I've never heard of.

The lane pops me out on the main road that runs through my suburb. It's a road that if travelled from end to end runs eight hundred kilometres all the way to Sydney. I dash across in front of cars, risking a toot, pretending I'm in New York or London. The entrance to the rooftop bar is next to the pub and I dip into the staircase.

In front of me are three young people clambering the three flights of stairs to the sunlight. They are revealing their stories of their fathers: brutal, cruel, selfish. Three steps up, a girl turns to me, her hair long and dark, and asks if I have 'daddy issues' too.

'No,' I say, pleased I can tell her that these days my dad and I are patched up and functioning.

Act Three: Other Scenes

My dad and I haven't always been this close. In the past I took Mum's side when they argued because she was better at eliciting my allegiance than he was. After Mum died, Dad and I wobbled. Her death broke me. She had been my strongest ally and suddenly I was anchorless. Then I saw a psychologist who shifted things for me and I let my childhood feelings go.

I slowly drifted back to Dad, who I could appreciate differently now that Mum was gone. He is not the man he was when she was alive. He is open and curious, engaged and present. He listens to my children explain the shifting language of how we think about gender and tries to understand. He doesn't judge and he is always in my corner. When I'm on the radio each fortnight, talking books, he listens. He's the only one who regularly does, texting me after with a commentary about my performance. He's proud, bursting with it, like I'm not middle-aged, but still a child needing his attention.

My car once broke down on a freeway in the countryside. I rang Dad from a phone box and he drove miles to tow me all the way home. He would always turn up when I needed him to. Not in a saviour way. Just in a solid, dependable, that's-what-you-do-for-your-kids way.

I don't tell the girl with the long dark hair all of that. Just that he is my only living parent and it matters that we are close now.

She tells me I'm lucky. She hates her father. Her words are flippant and loose.

I find myself wondering what he did to her. And if I wasn't in need of a drink, I'd quiz her, find out more. I think she'd tell me everything on that narrow staircase in the seedy late-afternoon light.

The boy up front slings his arm around his other friend and says, 'It's a club that you're fortunate to join because nobody needs a dad.'

I think about my children and how they would react to those words.

We spill out into the noise of the rooftop. The three friends peel away and find a table, still laughing and confessing their family stories.

I look around, scanning faces to find my tribe. I sit down at the long bench and tell them about the staircase conversation. We joke that my friend should call his band 'Daddy Issues' because it's a band of four dads who met when their children were at primary school. A band that plays loud, obscure punk songs. We agree it's the perfect name and I feel clever for a second.

Everyone around us is happy on the rooftop. It's a Friday and the drinks are cheap. I go to the bar and order myself a Campari and soda, while two women older than me tell me the sweet potato chips are the finest in the land. Instead, I eat one of the pieces of fried cauliflower ordered before I arrived; it's cold in my mouth.

My friends are a couple. I am just me. They are a couple who socialise together and invite me along. I'm grateful to be included. We wait for the others to arrive. Another couple and one half of one, balancing the numbers a little.

I'm often the only single person now at a table. It's harder sometimes when it's just me meeting with women friends, giving the illusion of us all being alone, but knowing they are mostly returning home to someone. And I am not.

Act Three: Other Scenes

Now I realise how often I failed my single-parent friends in the past because I didn't understand the precarious place where you are everything.

But I am lucky too. My friends are generous and inclusive. They make sure I am not alone on days that matter. And my kids and I are often invited into other people's families and we take up our place at their table, relieved that it's not just us in this new-found form of family. I'm often struck by the kindnesses I am shown – the offer of a meal when I am busy with work, the sharing of a holiday house, the willingness to look after my children when I need time away. My friends have surely saved me these past years.

When the wife of a man I know dies of cancer, I turn up to the funeral, taking a seat next to my friend in the chapel where Aidan used to sing sometimes. I didn't know her well, but he's a mess. I hear about how he builds her coffin in his woodsmith's studio.

The service is not religious, but the building is, and I find myself thinking about the two people I've farewelled and the unorthodox spaces we have used: Aidan in a live music venue and my mum at the organic nursery down the road.

At a funeral early on in our relationship for one of his siblings, I took Holy Communion without knowing what it was. I stood and lined up for the body of Christ, eating the Host and sipping from the Cup of Life. Afterwards, Aidan grilled me and I had to admit I didn't know what it was nor what it meant. He laughed and explained it to me. From then on, I sat silent through every other Catholic funeral I had to attend.

★

I don't go to the drinks after the service for the woman who has just died. Instead, I sneak away, knowing I have a leave pass because of my own grief.

A few months go by and someone invites me to a dinner that the widowed man will be at. I don't want to talk loss and loneliness. I don't want to be paired with another in the same boat as me. My friend understands when I say no. She gets it and I'm relieved I don't have to explain. But I worry that this will be my lot: dinners with couples where conversations are skirted because people remember, or dinners where I'm seated next to others who have lost too.

My dad re-partnered two years after my mum died. And they are together still. There's a kindness between them, something tender in the way they talk to each other and tease. He often tells me how much he loves her.

When he has emergency brain surgery, it is his partner who calls me. We head for the hospital together, sharing our time in the ICU, understanding where we both fit in his life. She is strong and respectful, and I admire her patience with my dad and her gentle way of coaxing him along. We laugh as he begs the nurse for a glass of wine to celebrate his eightieth birthday in the ICU ward. I tell him he's dreaming. No alcohol after brain surgery. I buy him fresh underwear and pyjamas that will be too large on his small frame. He tells me how great the food is.

There is something so alive about him in this moment: his head with staples in two thick lines, yet he is sparkling with light.

Act Three: Other Scenes

My kids come to see him, wary perhaps of yet another hospital procedure, but they laugh with him, enjoying his performance as he shows them the screen where he orders meals.

He tells me about his plans to travel next year with his partner, and in the next breath he tells me that he negotiated a lower price to pay the surgeon. I laugh at the idea of him lying on the gurney, moments before the anaesthetic hit his system, haggling. He is not done yet. My dad.

It is now nearly three years for me since becoming 'a one' and I cannot imagine dating. My daughter tells me I'm not allowed to start until she leaves home. My son jokes while we watch the reality TV series *First Dates* that one of the contestants is a little like me. I complain at the comparison given how much older she is, believing myself wrinkle-free and less saggy than I am. My son thinks I might like to date a man like the one she is paired with. I throw a cushion at him and tell him I'm not interested. But he laughs.

A couple of friends have broached the topic and asked me about dating again. Someone jokingly enquired at a book launch if I was 'getting any'. I didn't know what to say.

I dream of sex sometimes, with men I know and some I don't. My body is on the verge of wanting, but then it stops, like an engine that won't turn over.

Aidan told me repeatedly before he died that he wanted me to feel free to be with someone else. Like I needed his permission. Like it was all about him. If he hadn't been trapped in that bed, incapable of moving, I might have told him to *fuck off*. We might have fought about it in that way we had, where we wrestled with words and usually ended up agreeing. Instead, I put it down to the medication, but I know it wasn't that. Perhaps he was trying to be part of whatever came next for me. Another relationship. Casual sex. Or maybe he was trying to remove any guilt I might feel if it happened.

One weekend I go away to a writers' festival interstate. There are parties and conversations, a sort of freedom I haven't had for a long time. There is sunshine and my arms are bare. I hear writers talking about their work. I see people I haven't seen since Aidan died and they tell me how sorry they are. But I am not here for that. I am not here for the past. I want the sweeping moments of now, the one-more-drink, the too-loud-laugh, the momentary fleeting grin of a stranger.

I don't call home as much as usual. I am not thinking about that version of me.

I barely sleep for three nights, starting the day with coffee and ending with wine. I leap into the freezing cold pool on the second floor of the hotel at six in the morning.

My body is waking up.

My friend calls it 'the perimenopausal horn' and I laugh at the description. It sounds about right. I'm suddenly aware of the charge in the air and I wonder what would happen if I had one more night.

Scene Thirteen: Company

It's one of those Melbourne days where rain swirls from nowhere and falls straight down, causing roads to flood and cars to slide. One of those days that Aidan loved most. He said it was his Irish heritage making him long for the grey and the miserable. But I think he just liked being indoors, with an excuse to have the heater going, the coffee pot percolating and the morning starting slowly.

The rain arrives just as my son is leaving for school with his bike helmet and bag. He pauses near the front door, lingers just long enough for me to rise from the couch where I sit in my gym pants and sweaty t-shirt. I grab the car key and slide my feet into a pair of black sandals that wait in the hall. We are outside in the street before we speak. He tells me to unlock the car so he can run, avoiding the worst of the rain. I trundle behind, not hurrying, but dodging the growing puddles.

The roads are jammed with cars. We spy someone he knows who is sheltering under a tree at the side of the park, waiting for the worst to pass.

'I can pick them up,' I say to my son, but he points out the bike and we both know it won't fit in our tiny car that is already storage for the overflowing bags and boxes of stuff meant for somewhere else.

We keep driving, avoiding the worst of the water gathering at the side of the roads and making it hard to steer. I remember the official warnings about not driving through floodwater: 'It only takes ten centimetres of water for your car to be out of control', or something like that. I try to remember the exact words, but I can't, and then I worry that it's five centimetres and not ten and surely the mass ahead of me is at least that.

There's an army of SUVs behind me, with lights brighter than mine, who are unsympathetic to my low-lying car, so I drive on. We turn off the radio and turn up the windscreen wipers. They shudder trying to keep up.

By the time we park outside school, the bell is sounding and my son has seconds to race to his class before he is marked late. He fiddles with the umbrella and gives up, holding the half-open spokes over his head as he clambers out of the car. Rain leaks in as he reaches for his bag. There's a last-minute 'I love you' tossed back at me as he leaves.

I watch him dash for the open doors and disappear.

Driving home, I know I could stop by the side of the road and wait for the worst of it to pass, but there's a freedom that comes after my son is safely tucked away at school and so I keep driving, slowly, so slowly, creeping because I'm scared of the storm.

Act Three: Other Scenes

There's no thunder but a slice of lightning brightens the sky as I turn onto the road that leads to our place. By the time I find a park outside our apartment, the rain has nearly stopped and the air smells crisp and fresh like it's just been cleaned.

My daughter is getting up as I walk in. She's wearing her boyfriend's singlet and her dad's pyjama pants that we've all had a turn at wearing. She is slicing bread and making iced coffee as she does every morning. We chat about books while I get changed out of my gym clothes and into black jeans and the top I wore yesterday. I borrow her deodorant because my natural one has stopped working on me.

While she eats, she tells me her new co-worker is a reader and a film watcher and one of those people who understands her references without explanation.

I think about how long it's been since I've felt that. Aidan was that. I have friends who are too, but Aidan knew all of it – the life moments, the family stories – he didn't need context.

I steal her crusts because that's what I have for breakfast most days and then pack my bag while she checks the tram timetable for me. She tells me to run if I don't want to wait twenty minutes for the next one.

I kiss her goodbye and she smells like butter and vegemite, and I think how reassuring it is. There's something to be said for routines.

The cat chases my feet as I walk towards the front door for the third time that morning. I call out to my daughter to put the washing out when she has a chance. And maybe take down the rubbish. She yells back that it's her brother's turn.

I let the door slowly close behind me and I take the stairs.

My knees creak as I step down, tensing from the morning's squats. I realise I forgot my umbrella and hope the rain eases.

To finish this book, I have been visiting the state library in the city. It's quiet there and I can disappear into the aisles of books and the students working. Nobody cares about me and I feel freer than I have in some time.

I divide my day into sections. The morning bursts where I write without stopping until I treat myself with a coffee. The second session of my day is before lunch, when I try to clean up the mess I made earlier and accept that it's not the brilliant writing I had hoped for. And after lunch, which is unpredictable. Some days, I stare at people around me, trying to imagine what they are working on, hoping to glimpse their computer screens while my own goes to sleep because of lack of use. Other days, I edit my work or find myself distracted by something I looked up on the internet.

Today as I enter the library, I see a woman I know a little from my apartment block. She smiles and we chat, and I discover that she is a volunteer here once a fortnight. She asks me what I am working on and I tell her about this book, but I mumble and downplay it because I'm still unsure of my place outside being a children's writer.

She asks me where I work when I come to the library and I tell her I like the hard wooden chairs in the dome room. They stop me from procrastinating too much. She asks if I've ever worked in the Ian Potter Queen's Hall and I tell her I haven't.

We walk up the stairs together, she's leading slightly as she tells me why she likes this space most. The air isn't as cold as it can

Act Three: Other Scenes

be in the reading room. And because it is upstairs, people don't wander through so often, so you could hide out without anyone ever knowing you were there.

The automatic doors open to the long thin room with rich yellow-hued lighting and an ornate ceiling. I see immediately that she is right. It's a quiet space with large desks and more comfortable cloth-covered chairs. I thank her and find a table to park my things.

Before she leaves, she asks if any of my books are in the library because the young adult section is here, near the table I have chosen. I laugh, doubtful, but glance towards some of the titles on display, seeing names I recognise.

My hair is still damp from the drizzle of rain as I left the tram and I unpack my bag onto the table, discovering the umbrella I didn't think I had. I also spy one lost chocolate freckle from a packet my daughter brought home from the chocolate shop where she now also works. My son must have left it for me when he raided my stash. I try to tip it out of the packet, but the plastic is crinkly and I worry about the sound. Now I've started, I must eat the chocolate because, if I don't, I won't be able to work.

I tip the bag up and the brightly coloured hundreds and thousands left behind from other freckles scatter onto my hand. I eat them quickly, perhaps enjoying this single freckle more than I have ever enjoyed a chocolate.

I prepare to write but find myself looking back at the display books in the young adult section. I leave my things and move up and down the aisles looking for *W*.

I find my friends' books.

Williams.

Wood.

I've gone too far for me. I shuffle backwards, bent over, hopeful. And there I am.

Weetman.

Four of my books clumped together, representing years of work.

The Edge of Thirteen
The Secrets We Keep
The Secrets We Share
Sick Bay

Their spines are crisp and solid. I touch them gently with my fingertips and then return to my table.

I smile to myself. This is the State Library of Victoria. A place of wonder.

I start to write. This chapter. About who I am now.

A writer.

A mother.

A middle-aged woman who likes chocolate freckles and walking in the rain.

When I come back after lunch, two people have taken my large table. And because they are a two and I am a one, I look around for somewhere else to sit. There is another large table opposite me. Another six-seater.

This time I settle, not in front of the young adult section, but now at the feet of the Australian poetry and drama section. Hundreds of thin volumes dot the shelves.

I don't wait. I leap up and start searching.

Act Three: Other Scenes

F.

I find it.

Fennessy.

Aidan's final play.

The Heartbreak Choir

It's the only volume of his work they have, which surprises me because so many have been published as texts.

And then I realise that our books are in the same location on the aisles but on opposite sides of the room. They are only metres apart. Like they are preparing to face each other for a dance. Or a kiss.

I lift his play out, carry it back to my table and place it next to me while I open my laptop and start to work.

He is gone but his work has not. He is here in this giant of a building, this institution of thinking, where our daughter studied for her year twelve exams, where I've written books with my friend, where my son used to come as a child just to spy Ned Kelly's armour.

He is here. With me.

Epilogue: In the Gaps

It has taken me a long time to start missing the well version of you, but recently you have started to return to me. Little moments from before. The hot water bottles you filled each night to slip in our beds. The way you cleared the table after a long dinner, stacking plates to clean in the kitchen so the house would be set for morning. The sound of your voice when you sang. Your easy laugh when your friends were with you, trading jokes and insults. Returning home to find a new piece of furniture you'd salvaged from the street. Your refusal to wear sandals.

For so long you were the body in the bed, catheter attached, pills being swallowed every hour or two. You were the legs that wouldn't stand. The eyes that kept crying. The rage that bubbled up with the steroids they were giving you for the inflammation.

You were the dying. And I was not. And we split with that. One of us still planning for more days. And one of us who could not.

It's hard to part with the moments from that time. Hard to let them go because they were forged in sadness or anger or frustration. But they were not you. Just a patchwork of oxycodone and chemo, pain and confusion.

Only recently have I also started missing your potential and not just who you were. The sparring arguments that you had with our daughter that you will not have with our son. The gigs you would have taken them to. The holidays we would have had. All the conversations that will never happen, the jokes we won't hear, the plays you won't write.

On your computer you have many half-written works. I don't know what you want me to do with them. Single scenes, half an act, a few sketched ideas. All that unfinished storytelling.

Reading over a script you were writing set backstage in a rehearsal room where the cast is grappling with *King Lear*, I can hear your sometime rants about wishing that Shakespeare was relegated to the past. Do you remember? New Australian work should feature firmly in all mainstage seasons in this country. Or something like that. All the unsuspecting people you sat next to at dinner parties where you railed in detail about what was wrong with the industry.

At the time I may have yawned, but now I miss that. Your passion, your anger, your love of theatre. It was the constant in your life.

I think of all that has changed in the years since you've died. The apartment we now live in. The height of our son. The fact our daughter is an adult.

Epilogue

Your last play has been performed here and overseas. You've been nominated for awards, but you didn't win. You'd probably have something to say about that too.

And I'm sorry about the apartment. There are cobwebs. The windows aren't clean. I rarely make my bed. A pile of stuff sits permanently in our corridor waiting to be taken to the op shop, but it never is.

I'm sorry I killed your plant. And broke the coffee machine.

I know I should make more of an effort but I'm not you.

I have stories to tell you. Arguments to tackle. Ideas to share. Things that would make you laugh. I want to cook pea and ham soup now that it's getting cold, with pea you made yourself. A tired joke that never failed to make me smile.

Sometimes at night I still wait to hear your boots on the floorboards in a place you never lived in. I wait for the clink of the metal on your belt buckle as your pants hit the floor. I wait for the smell of bacon cooking, the sound of your voice as you ring me so many times a day, the touch of your arms as you pull me in for a hug.

Sometimes I miss you so much that I'm angry that I'm here and you're not, and you can avoid getting the oven fixed and the worry of the unpaid bills and if there will be work next month.

Sometimes I just want to take a minute, a breath, a pause, and stop. Before I forget you. Before your voice leaves my head. Before the only memories I have are from photographs.

The kids thought they saw you the other day in the street. It was your socks that did it. Those ugly thick white socks you bought from an op shop that you used to wear pushed down around the ankles with a pair of scuffed brown leather shoes and shorts. They followed the socks but it wasn't you.

We drive over train track crossings and I expect to hear 'Ding, ding, ding!' in your joking voice, and sometimes one of us says it for you.

And where are the chicken chips? The cupboard has none.

The missing is in the gaps where you should be. My sentences that you should finish. The anecdotes you should be telling. The plays you should be writing.

That's where I look for you. In the gaps.

Author's Note

I acknowledge the traditional owners and custodians of the land on which I wrote this book, the land of the Kulin Nation. I acknowledge that sovereignty was never ceded – it always was, and always will be, Aboriginal land.

Writing a memoir sometimes means treading on toes and hopefully I've trodden lightly. I know it hasn't always been easy for my kids, and at times I'm sure they would prefer I was anything other than a writer. I want to thank them for their humour, their frankness and their love. Without them I'd be lost. And also living alone with the cat, who doesn't like me very much at all.

I started writing this in lockdown while Aidan was still alive. I didn't know then that it would become something publishable. I thought at the time that it was just my way of processing what was happening. It was my agent who suggested later that I shape it into a book about all the ways we face loss and grief in our lives.

It took me nearly three years to finish, and I am aware of the privilege in writing like that. Early on, Creative Victoria gave me a much-needed grant that meant I could spend a chunk of time just thinking and plotting. Usually, I write quickly and to a strict deadline, but this book was written with space, and without knowing if anyone would want it once it was finished.

Writing this book has required enormous support from writer and non-writer friends. Friends who read the early tentative drafts and gave excellent feedback, friends who read the later

Author's Note

tentative drafts and gave excellent feedback, and friends who just kept me sane while I grieved and wrote. Thank you all for the conversations, the walks, the phone calls, the meals, the flowers, the financial help, and the love that you have shown our little family that has helped us to heal.

Having a community of people who know us and knew Aidan means he is still part of things somehow. I didn't really understand how important my community was until he died and, now that I know, I'm never leaving.

A book takes a village and I've scored a brilliant one. Thanks to my agent, Allison Hellegers, for suggesting this become a book in the first place. Thanks to everyone at UQP for everything you do: publisher Aviva Tuffield for having such faith; editor Kristy Bushnell for having such patience; project editors Cathy Vallance and Ian See for all the finessing; marketing and publicity legends Sarah Valle, Jean Smith and Sally Wilson; sales manager Kate Lloyd; designer Josh Durham; rights manager Erin Sandiford; and proofreader Vanessa Pellatt. And thanks to artist Bren Luke for your perfect cover illustration.

When Aviva asked me for my wishlist of endorsers, I didn't dare dream they would agree. A huge thanks to Annabel Crabb, Benjamin Law, Melina Marchetta, Jacinta Parsons and Myfanwy Warhurst for your generous time and support.

Aidan taught me how to recognise a good story, how to take my writing seriously and how to trust my voice. I hope reading some of his words will make you want to seek out his plays. They are as special as he was.

Thanks for reading.